Palgrave Studies in European Union Politics

Series Editors

Michelle Egan
School of International Service,
American University
Washington, District of Columbia, USA

Neill Nugent
Manchester Metropolitan University
Manchester, United Kingdom

William E. Paterson
Aston University
Birmingham, United Kingdom

Following on the sustained success of the acclaimed European Union Series, which essentially publishes research-based textbooks, Palgrave Studies in European Union Politics publishes cutting edge research-driven monographs. The remit of the series is broadly defined, both in terms of subject and academic discipline. All topics of significance concerning the nature and operation of the European Union potentially fall within the scope of the series. The series is multidisciplinary to reflect the growing importance of the EU as a political, economic and social phenomenon.

More information about this series at
http://www.springer.com/series/14629

Patricia Mindus

European Citizenship after Brexit

Freedom of Movement and Rights of Residence

palgrave
macmillan

Patricia Mindus
Philosophy Department
Uppsala University
Uppsala, Sweden

Palgrave Studies in European Union Politics
ISBN 978-3-319-51773-5   ISBN 978-3-319-51774-2 (eBook)
DOI 10.1007/978-3-319-51774-2

Library of Congress Control Number: 2017930933

Printed on acid-free paper

This Palgrave Macmillan imprint is published by Springer Nature
The registered company is Springer International Publishing AG
The registered company address is: Gewerbestrasse 11, 6330 Cham, Switzerland

"[T]hat is the miracle of Union citizenship: it strengthens the ties between us and our States (in so far as we are European citizens precisely because we are nationals of our States) and, at the same time, it emancipates us from them (in so far as we are now citizens beyond States)"
AG Poiares Maduro, *Opinion* on the *Rottman* case (2010)

*"Un miracle, selon l'énergie du mot, est une chose admirable (…).
On exige donc que la doctrine soit appuyée par les miracles, et les miracles par la doctrine"*
Voltaire, *Dictionaire philosophique* (1764)

CONTENTS

CHAPTER 1

Introduction

Abstract The book aims to explain the problems faced by European citizens in the UK and by UK citizens residing in member states of the European Union (EU) after Brexit. Particular emphasis is laid on freedom of movement and rights relating to residence. A conceptually solid approach is suggested so as to disentangle the various aspects of the question. No matter its shape, Brexit will need to imply changing the territorial scope of application of the EU Treatises. This will bring changes to the personal sphere of validity of EU law. The citizenry is expected to shrink in size and change in composition, and some parts of it will be left in potentially vulnerable positions.

Keywords European citizenship · Brexit · United Kingdom · Freedom of movement · Right of residence · EU law

The referendum on 23 June 2016 triggered a wave of concern on matters political, constitutional, international and more. There are many issues surrounding the procedure of exiting, when the UK will do it, about the constitutionally legitimate procedure to do so, about the drafting techniques of the treaties, in parallel or subsequently, that Article 50 will require on exit and future relations, and how the Brexit withdrawal Treaty may be enforced, what happens if the UK changes its mind during the negotiations, and more.[1]

© The Author(s) 2017   1
P. Mindus, *European Citizenship after Brexit*, Palgrave Studies
in European Union Politics, DOI 10.1007/978-3-319-51774-2_1

The question asked here is: What are the consequences that Brexit may entail for the regulation of nationality and migration, taking into consideration European Union (EU) citizenship? The book investigates European citizenship after Brexit, in light of the functionalist theory, that is, a general theory that develops an epistemologically strong account of the concept of *status civitatis* (Mindus 2014a, b; Cuono 2015). Such a theoretically informed inquiry is warranted for a number of reasons and enables relevant policy suggestions.

As things currently stand, outcomes of negotiations cannot be foreseen. Focus here will be on determining what resources, if any, are available to the legal scholar regardless of what may happen in negotiations. Therefore, this study is made under the assumption of a non-negotiated withdrawal.

Many have, of course, pointed out the unlikelihood of non-negotiated withdrawal. Yet, I will operate under this assumption, or the assumption of a withdrawal treaty making no mention of free movement rights, which for the present purposes would amount to the same thing. I have chosen to operate under this assumption because the question of remedies in the absence of an agreement is relevant since there is no guarantee that any future agreement would have terms that are favourable to all affected groups and/or that any agreement would claim comprehensiveness. The political likelihood of determinate negotiational outcomes is therefore secondary to establishing the legal situation that would prevail in absence of agreements to come. Knowing what negotiations can do helps us assess the quality of the output of these.

So without engaging in predictions about what is likely to happen politically or in the negotiations, the book aims to explain the problems faced by European citizens in the UK and by British citizens resident in member states of the EU after Brexit. Particular emphasis is laid on freedom of movement and rights relating to residence. This allows the reader to understand the legal complexities affecting those who, on both sides of the UK border, have relied on free movement in making their life choices. The book suggests adopting a conceptually solid approach so as to disentangle the various aspects of the question because, no matter its shape, Brexit will need to imply changing the territorial scope of application of the EU Treatises.[2] This will bring changes to citizenship, that is, the 'personal sphere of validity of the legal order' (Kelsen 1945). The citizenry is expected to shrink in size and change in composition, and some parts of it will be left in potentially vulnerable positions.

The study presented here looks at what extra-negotiational legal resources are available for freezing rights of the people involved. Can rights be frozen? Which rights? Whose rights? Under what conditions? For how long? Sources of international law and EU law, including guidelines from lesser-known sources and doctrinal instruments, are taken into consideration. The conclusion is that some rights of some of the people involved will be frozen, but that the legal grounds for doing so suggests that Union citizenship is not what the European Court of Justice and most scholars claim it is.

Sources of international and EU law also help us answer the following question: Who gets to withdraw Union citizenship? It is a complex and debated issue. The various options are presented, discussed and the consequences of loss of Union citizenship are fleshed out, as well as the anticipated consequences for both the UK and for EU member states. Different venues for challenging the loss of status are also presented and discussed, as well as the options available for the EU to 'save' its status. Once the allocation of competence to withdraw European citizenship is established, we move on to looking at what limits there are to what the UK can do to protect itself against abuse of multiple citizenships and what member states are allowed to do to UK citizens resident in their territories.

The book is structured in seven chapters, including the present introduction. Chapter 2 presents the status of European citizenship and connected rights. Chapter 3 narrates the problem of legal uncertainty afflicting second country nationals in the UK and British citizens turning from expats to post-European third country nationals. The reader who feels comfortable in mastering the legal complexities affecting those who have relied on free movement in making their life choices can move on to the next chapter. Chapter 4 starts by explaining why a theoretically informed inquiry is needed and then moves on to describe the theory. It also delineates three ways in which it applies to Brexit. These three directions of inquiry are developed in the remaining part of the book. Chapter 5 focuses on the intension of Union citizenship: Which rights can be frozen? Chapter 6 determines the extension of Union citizenship: Who gets to withdraw the status? The key finding is that while member states are in principle free to revoke the status of Union citizen, former member states are not unbounded in stripping Union citizens of their acquired territorial rights. In the final chapter (Chapter 7) some conclusions as to the nature of Union citizenship are drawn, and policy suggestions concerning how to regulate matters pertaining to nationality and EU citizenship are summed up. The study offers performative evidence of the policy relevance of the general theory of citizenship that is sketched out in Chapter 4.

Acknowledgements are also due. A first draft was presented at the EUI Law Department in Fiesole, Florence in September 2016 and a second draft was presented at Uppsala Law Department Higher Seminar Series in Constitutional Law. I am grateful to comments and feedback received by Nehal Bhuta, Anna Cornell Jonsson, Marise Cremona, Fabrizio Esposito, Oliver Garner, Gábor Halmai, Hans-W. Micklitz, Sebastián Reyes Molina, Martin Scheinin, Marinius Jacobus Van der Brink and the other participants in the seminars, as well as the blind referees at Palgrave Macmillan. A special thanks goes to Mathilde Cohen and Marco Goldoni for their constant encouragement and comments on early drafts. The research presented here was conducted under the auspices of two research projects: The project entitled *Arbitrary Law-Making* (412-2012-725) sponsored by the Swedish Research Council and the project entitled *Civis Sum* that I direct as Wallenberg Academy Fellow (2015–2020) sponsored by the KAW Foundation. For those interested in our project, there is a website at civissum.eu. I wish to acknowledge the generous research support received from the Swedish Research Council, Knut and Alice Wallenberg Foundation and Uppsala University. This book, as much else, would not have seen the light had it not been for the enduring support of my family. A long summer by the sea provided the ideal setting.

It is dedicated to my favourite European citizen, Livia.

NOTES

1. See in general the 2016 debates on https://ukconstitutionallaw.org.
2. Articles 52 TEU and 355 TFEU which establishes the territorial scope of application of the Treaties, merely list each Member state *eo nomine*.

REFERENCES

Cuono, M. (ed.) (2015) 'Cittadinanza. Un dibattito a più voci', in *Materiali per una cultura giuridica*, 2.

Kelsen, H. (1945) *General Theory of Law and State*, Cambridge, MA: Harvard University Press.

Mindus, P. (2014) [2014a] 'Dimensions of Citizenship', 15 *German Law Journal* (5), available at https://static1.squarespace.com/static/56330ad3e4b0733dcc0c 8495/t/56b10a23c2ea51dd0e80a723/1454443052623/GLJ_Vol_15_No_05. pdf (last accessed 30 October 2016).

Mindus, P. (2014) [2014b] *Cittadini e no. Forme e funzioni dell'inclusione e dell'esclusione*, Florence: Firenze University Press.

CHAPTER 2

The Status of European Citizenship: An Overview

Abstract This chapter gives a swift overview of the workings and principal rights associated with European citizenship. Some insight into the historical evolution of the status is offered. The major entitlements are explained as well as important case-law. The aim is to provide an outline of the essentials of European citizenship for the purpose of understanding the arguments made in this book.

Keywords European citizenship · Brexit · United Kingdom · Freedom of movement · Right of residence · EU law · EU citizens' rights

The status of European citizenship was introduced in European law with the Maastricht Treaty in 1992. Let us see what steps were taken to establish this particular form of *status civitatis* that differs from the standard legal form of citizenship that we are used to consider equivalent to nationality. It is additional to having member state nationality. It entails a series of rights that nationals of member states would not enjoy if they were not European citizens. This confers a degree of independence to the content of the status. It is not, however, an autonomous status. Yet, member states are not fully autonomous in exercising discretion over who gets access to the status. This overview shows what makes European citizenship a *status sui generis* that is not constituted in the same way as nationality in unitary states or dual citizenship commonly found in federal systems. The aim of this chapter is

© The Author(s) 2017
P. Mindus, *European Citizenship after Brexit*, Palgrave Studies
in European Union Politics, DOI 10.1007/978-3-319-51774-2_2

not to present European citizenship in an exhaustive manner but to shed light on some key aspects of the status that are important for the arguments made in the book.

2.1 EU CITIZENSHIP: A BRIEF HISTORY

2.1.1 The Background

The first practical steps towards EU citizenship were taken in the 1970s (Maas 2007). Following the Paris Summit in October 1972, it was suggested that a European identity would be needed to deepen integration. More precisely, for the committee chairman, Xavier Ortoli, the lack of a European identity was one of the weaknesses of the European Community.[1] Following the summits in Copenhagen in 1973 and in Paris the following year, the issue of integration became more pressing. At the Copenhagen summit a document on European identity was drafted, in which, mostly in general terms, emphasis was laid on common cultural heritage. The political aim of strengthening integration between member states started taking shape during the next summit in Paris. It was suggested that the involvement in the integration process of the citizens of the member states could enhance a future European identity. From here came the idea of having a common *status civitatis*.

To be precise, at least since the 1960s, the idea of a European citizenship had been proposed on different occasions, albeit in a rather indefinite manner. For example, the vice president of the Commission Lionello Levi Sandri had argued for prioritising the free movement of persons over the free movement of goods as it would be a first step towards European citizenship. It was only in the course of the 1970s, in particular in the wake of the Paris Summit, that deepened integration started being spelled out in terms of citizenship. It resulted in the 1974 report on special rights by the Belgian Leo Tindemans. In this report it was recommended that certain rights should be attributed to the 'ressortissants' of the member states, that is, their nationals. They included the right to vote and stand in elections for the European Parliament and the establishment of a European passport, which would lead to the so-called passport policy.[2] This report, however, did not claim the rights in question to be of European citizens, but to be necessary for a 'Europe of citizens.'[3] Tindemans handed in the report on the 29th of December 1975 and the Commission started to look into the so-called question of special rights.[4]

Nevertheless, with the protection of special rights, a legal problem arose, given that European citizens would enjoy rights both in their state of origin and in their state of residence. European citizens, in other words, would not be subjected to the principle of naturalisation, then commonly applied, according to which one would lose one's original citizenship in case of naturalisation abroad. According to the Commission, in fact, there was a risk of reversed discrimination that would have resulted in EU citizens being more protected than the citizens of the host state. The result, unsurprisingly, was that the special rights policy had a rather limited impact.

Tindemans' ideas were later revived by the European Parliament that presented a series of resolutions on European integration, considering the possibility of ascribing special rights to citizens of member states. Mario Scelba presented a report entitled *Granting special rights to the citizenship of the community* before the Parliament in Strasbourg on the 16th of November 1977. Many practical implications were put on hold. Yet, universal suffrage was introduced in the election of the European Parliament in 1979, putting into a new light the phenomenon for which David Marquand coined the famous expression 'democratic deficit' (Marquand 1979). It was held that the institution of universal suffrage constituted an embryonic form of citizenship.

The still rather imprecise idea of European citizenship came to the fore again in February 1984, when, in preparation of the Fontainebleau inter-governmental conference, the European Parliament presented a draft Treaty on the European Union, in which explicit mention of European citizenship was made in terms similar to those later adopted. During the Fontainebleau summit on the 25th and 26th of June 1984, two commit-tees were established: the *ad hoc* committee on 'The Europe of Citizens' directed by Pietro Adonnino and another committee on 'Institutional Affairs' directed by James Dooge. The Adonnino Committee drafted two reports that focused on the objectives to be achieved respectively in the short and in the long run. They were presented to the European Council in Brussels in March 1985 and in Milan in June of the same year. The Adonnino report left no great signs on the Single European Act, an amending treaty signed in Luxembourg on the 17th of February 1986. Its preamble only makes a vague reference to European citizenship (Sébastien 1993).

It was only later, at the summit in Madrid on the 25th and 26th of June 1989, that the political will to introduce European citizenship became tangible. The heads of state gathered in the Spanish capital stressed how the European Community had failed to realise 'the Europe of citizens.' Following the Martin report from February 1990, the European Parliament called for a specific formulation of rights of European citizenship to be included in the future Treaty of Maastricht. A memorandum was written by the Belgian Foreign Minister Eysken suggesting the adoption of a uniform electoral procedure for the election of the European Parliament, in addition to the right to vote in local elections for all EU citizens. Nevertheless, it was first and foremost Spain that pushed in the direction of adopting the new *status civitatis* at Maastricht.

In a letter to the President of the European Council, dated the 4th of May 1990, the Spanish Prime Minister Felipe Gonzalez suggested instituting a form of supranational citizenship as a step towards a future political union. According to this scenario, nationals of member states resident in other states than the one of which they hold nationality should not be cast as privileged foreigners. Rather, they had to be granted rights that were classified as 'special basic rights,' 'new dynamic rights' and 'protective rights.' Leaving aside the merit of classification that, to some extent is reminiscent of that of T.H. Marshall (1950) then very much *en vogue*, it is interesting to note that the first category included the right to freedom of movement, freedom of residence, participation in political life in the place of residence, while social, environmental and cultural rights were listed under 'new rights' and the third category included the protection of the soon-to-be-instituted European citizens outside the Community. The Spanish memorandum came to play an important role in legal translation of these ideas into what we find in the Maastricht Treaty.

Shortly before the approval of the Treaty, at the special meeting of the European Council in Rome on the 27th and 28th of October 1990, a document was presented, in which European citizenship was understood to complement national citizenship, as a status attributed to those who already have the nationality of a member state. Following a new Spanish proposal from the 21st of February 1991, the idea began to circulate that defining the new status of European citizenship ought to be done by inserting a new title in the Treaty that the member states were now entering into. Issues relating to citizenship would, therefore, become a European policy. The political will to institute this new *status civitatis* was undeniably present at the time, but it was not until the Maastricht Treaty in 1992 that it was expressed in a legally binding text.

The Treaty establishing the European Community, better known as the Maastricht Treaty, ascribes a series of rights to citizens of the member states in the second part relating to *citizenship*: Articles. 18–21 TEC.[5] These establish, first of all, the right to free movement within the Union (Article 18 TEC; now TFEU Article 21), the right to vote and stand in elections both at the local and at the European level at the same conditions as first country nationals (Article 19 TEC; now TFEU Article 22). The Treaty also provides for the right to consular protection by member states in a third country where the right-holder's home state is not represented (Article 20 TEC; now TFEU Article 23), as well as the right to petition the European Parliament and to appeal the European ombudsman in cases of maladministration (Article 21 TEC; now TFEU Article 24). The final provisions of Article 22 TEC (now TFEU Article 25) provide that provisions may be adopted to strengthen or to add the rights laid down. It is thus an open list, a fact that is confirmed by other aspects too.

In fact, the rights listed in the second part of the Maastricht Treaty are not exhaustive of the status of the European citizen. This is not merely because of subsequent regulatory actions and later treatises, such as the Amsterdam Treaty, the Charter of Fundamental Rights of Nice or the Lisbon Treaty that have indeed added rights. It is so also because a series of legal positions have been ascribed to the European citizen in the case-law of the European Court of Justice. European citizens do not only have the rights listed under the heading relating to European citizenship in the treaties. These rights are also determined by case-law and by secondary legislation, that is, the legal acts, listed in Article 288 TFEU, including regulations, directives, decisions, recommendations and opinions.

2.1.2 A Farewell to Traditional International Law

European citizenship differs both from nationality in unitary states and from dual citizenship commonly found in federal systems (See, e.g. Bar-Yaacov 1961; Garot 1999; Hansen 2002; a comparison in Schönberger 2005). There are some structural reasons why.

Much emphasis was laid on the fact that, originally, the recognition of the individual's legal status in Community law did not differ from the legal status of subjects under international law (Jacobs 1976; Janis 1984; Nascimbene 1986; Lippolis 1994; Trevisani 1995; Cordini 2003). European law, however, broke with the tradition of international law, a matter which did not fail to impact on the legal status of individuals. The rules adopted by the Union are directly applicable to individuals and individuals may use, in some cases without reference to the state organs, the Court of Justice and the Court of First Instance. Rights can be claimed by the individual, not only against EU and member state institutions, but also against private persons and bodies.[6]

European law differs from international law in allowing direct individual access to the justice system. This fact provides some insight into what was considered to be the very point of introducing European citizenship: In the 'common provisions' in Title I, the parties to the Treaty are 'resolved to create a citizenship common to the nationals of their countries' and 'to strengthen rights of the nationals of their member states through the introduction of a citizenship of the Union.' The provision of rights is therefore a central aspect of European citizenship.

There are also other features of European citizenship that sets it apart from traditional constructs. There are reasons inherent to the very structure of the EU, and reasons inherent to the development of the case-law by the European Court of Justice:

First, the different legal positions associated with Union citizenship have a common principle: freedom from discrimination on grounds of nationality. In European law, nationality is not considered a relevant criterion for ascribing to individuals different legal positions, other things being equal, whereas differential treatment on grounds of nationality is a core feature of international law. In the second part of the consolidated versions of the Treaty on the Functioning of the European Union (TFEU), under the title 'Non-discrimination and Citizenship of the Union,' this principle is defined in the following terms: 'Within the scope of application of the Treaties, and without prejudice to any special provisions contained therein, any discrimination on grounds of nationality shall be prohibited' Article 18 TFEU (ex Article 12 TEC).

This is an atypical principle in this context. Traditionally, differential treatment on the grounds of nationality is precisely what *status civitatis* enables. The point of making the distinction between nationals and non-nationals is to allow differential treatment. Citizenship, or *status civitatis* to use the legal term of art, is a status that is recognised only by those having some privileged relationship with the community. Originally this relationship was conceived as a relationship of *perpetual allegiance* linking a territory's subjects to their ruler (Vanel 1951, p. 21) but, over the centuries, it came to be understood in national terms,[7] even though formally the introduction of the principle of nationality in international law occurs rather late.[8] Over the last couple of centuries – and with significant difficulties in colonial settings – the prevailing idea was that differential treatment on grounds of nationality did not equate to discrimination. To the contrary, nationality was admittedly considered to offer justification, or good reason, to treat individuals differently. It is on this backdrop that the right to non-discrimination in European law can be said to stand in discontinuity with this traditional assumption that most forms of *status civitatis* rely on.

Second, the case-law that the European Court of Justice has developed on matters relating to citizenship departed in significant ways from the standard elaborated in international law. In European law, formal recognition of the status trumps the so-called effectiveness principle which otherwise rules international law. Under international law, in particular with reference to Article 5 of the Hague Convention from 12th April 1930,[9] the principle of effectiveness applies to the resolution of questions of citizenship (See, e.g. Quadri 1936; Bastide 1956; Glazer 1956; Maury 1958; Weis 1979; Carrera Nunez and De Groot 2015). In the event of contested citizenship due to multiple nationalities, residence ought to be guiding in order to identify the legal regime that applies to the individual. This is done by verifying the person's so-called habitual residence. The principle of effectiveness was reiterated, and took on this form, following the famous *Nottebohm* ruling from 1955 by the International Court of Justice. Here is a summary of the famous case:

Friedrich Nottebohm was born in 1881 in Hamburg as a German citizen. In 1905, he emigrated to Guatemala, where he successfully ran his business. He maintained close ties both professionally and personally, with Germany and Liechtenstein, where his brother moved in 1931. Several family members naturalised in Guatemala, but Friedrich Nottebohm, fearing that Guatemalan citizenship would harm his business, moved to Liechtenstein in 1939 and applied for naturalisation. Here he obtained naturalisation *ex iure pecuniae* a month after the outbreak of war; a conflict that he would witness from a safe distance, that is from Guatemala. Being a German, he was arrested by US order in October 1943 and deported to the USA, where, without a trial, he was held for two years and three months while his belongings were confiscated and sold in Guatemala. After a series of appeals in Guatemalan courts, Nottebohm was able to obtain the diplomatic protection of Liechtenstein. In 1951, Liechtenstein presented an appeal before the international court of justice.

At the outset, it was necessary to determine whether Liechtenstein could grant its diplomatic protection to Nottebohm. In denying the existence of a legally significant bond with Liechtenstein, the Court, in line with already mentioned Hague Convention, gave a definition of citizenship based on the principle of effectiveness: 'nationality is a legal bond having as its basis a social fact of attachment, a genuine connection of existence.'[10] This definition is the one currently adopted in international law and it is known as the doctrine of genuine link.

It is this doctrine that the European Court of Justice distances itself from in establishing its case-law on Union citizenship. Its case-law departed from the principle of effectiveness with the *Micheletti* ruling.[11] Here are the facts of the case: This ruling concerned Mario Vicente Micheletti, an Argentine dentist holding an Italian passport *ex iure sanguinis* who was refused a permanent residence card from the *delegación del gobierno* of Cantabria in Spain in March 1990. The appeal was presented before the *Tribunal Superior de Justicia* in the same Spanish region, requiring the administrative decision to be cancelled, in addition to the recognition of his right to obtain the residence card, a *conditio sine qua non* for the exercise of the profession, and to request, for other family members, the issuance of the residence certificate. In a preliminary ruling procedure, the Spanish court raised the issue of a conflict between Community law and Article 9 of the Spanish Civil Code, under which – and in accordance with international law – in cases of multiple nationality, the citizenship that prevails is that of state in which the person had her former habitual residence before arrival on Spanish territory; in this case, Argentina. However, the judges in Luxembourg considered that the provisions of Community law precluded a member state from refusing to grant the benefit of 'community rights' to an individual in possession of both the nationality of a member state and that of a third country, on the sole basis that the member state did not recognise the person to be a second country national, that is, a person having the nationality of another member state.

Basically, under EU law, a member state may not decide who are to be considered as nationals of another member state and therefore no additional criteria can be added to assess citizenship, such as the genuine link doctrine: Merely having the nationality of a member state is sufficient to be recognised by the European legal system as a second country national (See, e.g. Borras Rodriguez 1993; Iglesias Buhigues 1993; Jessurun d'Oliveira 1993; Ruzié 1993; Carrascosa 1994).

Apart from the reasons mentioned, inherent to the structure of the EU and to the development of the case-law of the European Court of Justice, there is yet another reason for differentiating between European citizenship and common forms of *status civitatis*. It pertains to how the status was introduced into EU law. Indeed, at Maastricht, when the Treaty on the European Community was signed, a choice had been made about how to design the access gate to this new citizenship. The designers shaped the access gate so as to make European citizenship a derivative status. In a nutshell, there are 28 ways to access the status.

2.2   THE DERIVATIVE CHARACTER OF UNION CITIZENSHIP

European citizenship is a status that has a very specific character: It is derivative. A person gains access to the status by already having access to another status: that of national of a member state for the purposes of EU law. The Article 20 TFEU (ex Article 17 TEC) provides the following: 'Citizenship of the Union is hereby established. Every person holding the nationality of a Member State shall be a citizen of the Union. Citizenship of the Union shall be additional to and not replace national citizenship.' This position was reiterated by the Declaration no 2 that was annexed to the Treaty of Maastricht on nationality of a member state, according to which 'the question whether an individual possesses the nationality of a Member State shall be settled solely by reference to the national law of the Member State concerned.' So member states retain the competence to define criteria for acquisition and loss of their own nationality. Nationality of a member state is therefore a necessary criterion for the acquisition of European citizenship. This derivative nature of EU citizenship confers upon it the quality of a complementary status, different from dual citizenship status common in federal states.

An often-repeated claim is that the choice of instituting European citizenship in this derivative way, via member state legislation, was the easy way out from the political perspective. It was not the only option on the table. In the 1970s, for example, there had been suggestions linking the status of European citizenship to the principle of *ius soli*, bestowing a birth-right status upon those born in the EU.[12] In the Nineties this way appeared to be politically tortuous; thus the option of a derivative and complementary status. The cost of this option is that different legal norms appear to be coexisting in a non-subordinate manner. For some, EU law and domestic law would even constitute competing norms (e.g. Evans 1991).

To limit state discretion in this area would have required harmonisation of domestic legislation on acquisition and loss of nationality. The harmonisation of nationality laws is important if the point is to prevent possible conflicts between the different domestic laws, to limit the possibilities of states to indirectly influence common rules, or to limit states' possibilities to exercise discretion when granting access to European citizenship for third county nationals (Nascimbene 1998). No such harmonisation occurred spontaneously. However, some efforts in this direction were made outside the framework of the European Communities. As a result of the work of the Council of Europe, an international treaty was signed in Strasbourg on the 6th of November 1997: The European Convention on Nationality (Schade 1995; Sabourin 1999).

It is worth noticing that the wording of the Article 20 TFEU has changed in the course of time: European citizenship is not merely 'derivative' (Treaty of Maastricht) but then also 'complementary' (Treaty of Amsterdam) and, after the Treaty of Lisbon, EU citizenship is said to be 'additional' (Geogiadou 2015, p. xix). Consider also that the abovementioned declaration on nationality was removed from the annex of the TEU after entry into force of the Lisbon Treaty.

This change is, to a great extent, the reflection of the development of the case-law (e.g. *Rottman*), according to which EU member states are not unbounded in stripping their own nationals of nationality in ways that would violate Union law. To be precise, the question whether an individual possesses the nationality of a Member state is no longer settled *solely* by reference to national law. So whereas in determining loss of citizenship states need to take into account EU law, and in particular general principles of EU law (such as the principle of proportionality), it is safe to say that nationality laws of member states is the legal source *par excellence* that determines access to the status. So supranational scrutiny of state discretion in this area is increasing, but this does not imply that states do not have discretion in defining their citizenship policy. The same year the Treaty of Lisbon came into force, a court ruling by the authoritative German constitutional court confirmed this view. In its 2009 *Lissabon Urteil*, the *Bundesverfassungsgericht* ruled that citizenship laws are to be considered 'core sovereignty' (Mindus and Goldoni 2012).

The fact that member states control access to the status may seem straightforward, but it is also a source of intricacies: There are 28 access gates to the status. The choice of using mere lexical reference to Member State nationality laws in Article 20 leaves the *Herren der Verträge* (Masters of the Treatises), in principle, free to determine the access criteria. There are several consequences.

A first consequence is that even though it is often claimed that all nationals of member states are European citizens, it is more accurate to say that a Union citizen is a national of a member state *for the purposes of European law*. Member states aiming to deprive of rights certain minority groups among their citizens have been able to engage in the inelegant practice of bringing this kind of unilateral declarations on the meaning of nationality for the purposes of EU law.[13] Indeed, the design-choice made in Article 20 (ex Article 17 TEC) left member states free to influence indirectly the personal scope of application of Community legislation through the application of their nationality laws. This explains why despite the fact that Article 20 provides that the citizen of a member state is also a Union citizen, there are citizens of member states that are not European citizens: e.g., the inhabitants of Faro Islands. The people of the Faro Islands are Danes but not EU citizens. The Danish government added a protocol specifying that 'the Danish nationals' of the islands were not 'nationals for the purposes of Community law.'[14] In sum, nationality of a member state is a necessary, albeit insufficient, criterion for acquisition of Union citizenship. To be sufficient, absence of unilateral declarations on the meaning of nationality for the purposes of EU law is required.

The design-choice also implies that – since we are in a setting in which no additional criteria may be added, following the break with the genuine link doctrine (see previous section) – member states are obliged to accept as second country nationals those who hold citizenship of any other member state, even though the first member state has no say in who gets to enjoy the status of national in that second state. Consider that as a result of the Spanish option right for the children of former Spanish nationals born in Spain (Art. 20 of the Spanish Civil Code), Fidel Castro could opt for European citizenship without moving from Havana (De Groot 2004, p. 7). No member state except Spain has a say on this matter.

Another puzzling case that has been discussed, and that might have some traction in a post-Brexit scenario, is this: What would happen if a member state would naturalise a significant part of the population of a state, which is not a member of the Union, without first consulting Brussels? For example, what happens if the Netherlands were to grant Dutch citizenship to the entire population of Surinam (De Groot 2004, p. 7)? It is not always clear what European law requires in relation to citizenship. What would have been the reaction of the Commission and the member states if Cyprus had not been accepted as a member and Greece would have granted citizenship to all Cypriots of Greek origin (Kotalakidis 2000, p. 299)?

Finally, mention ought also to be made of the fact that one of the parameters of representation in the Union is member states' population size. Depending on how population is defined (residents, EU citizens, nationals...), population size changes. It is susceptible of fluctuating considerably. Consider the fact that Greece, Hungary, Ireland but also Italy and Spain have a considerable number of expatriated citizens, while in other countries there is a significant presence of third country nationals. The relative 'weight' of the member state within the Union depends, albeit in a mediate way, on how access to nationality in these different countries is regulated and on how nationality law and immigration policies are designed. There is leeway for gerrymandering here.

Leaving the choice of designing the access gate to domestic law-makers might have been the easy way out in 1992, but today it seems to raise a lot of questions. Unclearness, in various forms, hoovers above the construct and specifically around the implications surrounding the derivative character of European citizenship. Much clearer are, however, the entitlements associated with the status.

2.3   ENTITLEMENTS CONNECTED TO THE STATUS

What holds EU citizenship rights together is the principle of non-discrimination on grounds of nationality (Art. 18 TFEU). The entitlements connected to EU citizenship share the assumption that the nationality a person holds is irrelevant for the purpose of enjoying the rights attributed by the Union. In this sense, European citizens are equal before EU law in their citizens' rights.

Over the years, we have witnessed an extension, or development, of rights in a two-fold way. Since its inception, the EU citizen has been subjected to a process of extension of both the *number* of rights and of the *personal scope* of the rights associated with it.

In the original Maastricht Treaty from 1992, the entitlements associated with European citizenship consisted of the following:

- The right to free movement and residence throughout the EU (and the right to work)

- Electoral rights (active and passive) to the European Parliament in any member state
- Local electoral rights (active and passive) in the EU state of residence, under the same conditions as the nationals of that state
- The right to consular protection abroad by any member state if there are no diplomatic or consular authorities from the citizen's home state
- The right to petition the European Parliament
- The right to petition the Ombudsman

The treatises that followed have added entitlements: The Amsterdam Treaty from 1997 added the right to address the EU in any official language and to receive a reply in that same language (Art. 24). This is a right that de facto will not be challenged by Brexit since other member states use English as official language. The Nice Charter, or Charter of Fundamental Rights of the European Union, from 2000 added the right to access documents from the European Parliament, the Council and the Commission (Art. 15) and the right to good administration (Art. 41). This Charter, even though authoritative, was not recognised as binding law until it was incorporated into the Treaty of Lisbon in 2009.

The major innovation that the Treaty of Lisbon added to the list of entitlements associated with Union citizenship was, however, another: The European Citizens' Initiative (Art. 11 TEU & Art. 24 TFEU), according to which EU citizens, representative of a cross-national opinion, present thus in several member states, can suggest to the Commission that it activate its legislative function on a particular matter. To activate a citizens' initiative, it is necessary that one million EU citizens, coming from at least seven member states, sign the initiative. Once it is activated, the Commission may decide to propose legislation as a result of it.

Entitlements have not only become more numerous, but they have also come to be interpreted as covering a higher number of persons and situations. This is largely due to the activity of the European Court of Justice, which has often extended the personal scope of entitlements. Generally speaking, the case-law has often taken on a kind of avant-gardism in pushing EU citizenship beyond the merely economically motivated concept.[15] Many are nonetheless unimpressed by its success in doing so. Without any claim to exhaustiveness, key rulings in which the Luxembourg Court played an active role include the following.

In the ruling *Rudy Grzelczyk* (C-184/99), the court declared that 'EU citizenship is destined to be the fundamental status of nationals of the Member States.' Non-economically active citizens had restricted rights to residence because of secondary law. In 1999 the ruling *Baumbast* (C-413/99) established that residence rights derive directly from the EU Treaty. Secondary legislation can limit this right but only in observance of the principle of proportionality. In the ruling *Zhu & Chen* (Case C-20/02), it was found that primary caretakers of minor EU citizens have a residence right: more precisely, it was found that denying residence to the third country national mother of a minor EU citizen 'would deprive the child's right of residence of any useful effect.' In *Ruiz Zambrano* (Case C-34/09) the Court supplemented the protection of the status of Union citizenship with the requirement that the substance of rights attached to the status be enjoyed:

> Article 20 TFEU precludes national measures which have the effect of depriving citizens of the Union of the genuine enjoyment of the substance of the rights conferred by virtue of their status as citizens of the Union. A refusal to grant a right of residence to a third country national with dependent minor children in the Member State where those children are nationals and reside, [. . .] has such an effect.

The court resorted to the 'substance' of European citizenship to ground the entitlement of a third country national to reside and work in Belgium as the father care-taker of two children who had been born nationals of Belgium in order to avoid statelessness that would have followed from being born by Colombian nationals who did not reside in Colombia (Colombia being a country applying *ius soli* quite strictly). However, the genuine substance doctrine has a quite limited *ratio decidendi* and is not likely to be applied broadly. Recently, the Court of Justice seems to have taken a more restrictive view: in *Dano* (Case C-333/13), through a restrictive interpretation of existing legislation, so-called benefit tourism was ruled out, by providing that 'persons exercising their right of residence should not, however, become an unreasonable burden on the social assistance system of the host Member State.'

A highly significant ruling for the arguments made in the following chapters is *Janko Rottman v. Freistaat Bayern* (Case C-315/08), illustrated in Chapter 6. Here it suffices to say that the case regarded loss of EU citizenship. The Court of Justice concluded that 'a citizen of the Union who is faced with a decision withdrawing his [citizenship], and placing him (...) in a position capable of causing him to lose the status conferred by Article 17 EC [Article 20 TFEU] and the rights attaching thereto falls, by reason of its nature and its consequences, within the ambit of European Union law.'[16] Since *Rottman*, member states are subjected to the general principles of European law in matters such as loss of Union citizenship. This means that member states are not unbounded in denationalising or imposing loss of *status civitatis*. This, to some, is a first crack in the idea that nationality law belongs to the field of 'core sovereignty' to use the phrasing of the German constitutional Court.

Some of the rights we are dealing with here were recognised before being proclaimed as rights associated with Union citizenship. For instance, the right to petition was first introduced into the European Coal and Steel Community in 1953. With the exception of electoral rights, the rights associated with Union citizenship are to a considerable extent a systematisation of already recognised entitlements. This is true for freedom of movement, the right of residence and the right of petition.

Do notice also that non-discrimination on the grounds of nationality applies independently of residence on Union territory. This means that, given that Article 20 TFEU does not make any reference to residence, the personal scope of European citizenship cannot be limited with reference to residence, as shown in *Eman & Sevinger*.[17] This has some importance here because it implies that Brexit cannot affect non-territorial rights of EU citizens as such, but only those rights the exercise of which is strictly territorial, most notably protections linked to freedom of movement.

The entitlements listed above are the major rights associated with European citizenship in the Treaties. British nationals, having no other member state nationality to rely on, and who are residing in the UK, would effectively be deprived of these rights in a non-negotiated Brexit scenario. They would lose rights associated with freedom of movement and residence, voting rights for the elections of the European Parliament, consular protection by another member state, right to adhere to European citizens' initiatives. Jurisprudentially developed protections, such as the right to export benefits and entitlements tied to nationality to a host member state[18] and the right not to be burdened, or discriminated for having exercised the freedom to move,[19] are entitlements that would also be lost together with the status of Union citizen.

British citizens, without a second member state nationality, who reside in another member state, will also lose these rights, but they will not – differently from British citizens in the UK – lose rights associated with EU citizenship whose personal scope is over-inclusive in respect of having the nationality in a member state. Some rights associated with European citizenship are recognised to all *residents*, not to all having the nationality of a member state. Entitlements that have this characteristic include the right to petition Parliament and the Ombudsman, the right to access documents from European Parliament, Council and Commission and the right to good administration. UK nationals in the Union would retain these rights also as third country nationals. Moreover, they will lose voting rights in local elections in many member states, but not all since some countries allow non-national franchise.

Special mention needs to be made of the right to freedom of movement. It is often cast as the core of the EU citizens' rights or the most significant right. It is a transnational right, linked to the crossing of borders. While other rights connected to EU citizenship can be exercised *in loco* by static EU citizens, free movement presupposes the crossing of borders by mobile EU citizens. It immediately follows from the so-called four freedoms. When it was framed as a right of the European citizen at Maastricht, the innovative character laid in the extension of the personal scope of a right that already existed. In fact, the EEC Treaty attributed the right of free movement only to certain categories of workers; more specifically, to employees (Art. 39–42 TEC), self-employed (Art. 43–48 TEC) and service providers (Art. 49–55 TEC). In the Nineties, the personal scope was extended to include also potential workers, such as students, and those benefitting from services, such as pensioners. A person's economic ability provided the reason for the limitation of the personal scope of the right to free movement. Nevertheless, free movement significantly extended over the years, first by effect of the case-law, and then by means of legislation. This change relegated economic activities to a secondary role in the interpretation of Community law and consequently the number of categories admitted to freedom of movement increased.

Today, freedom of movement and residence is not an entitlement strictly linked to Union citizenship. Its *ratio personae* is both over- and under-inclusive. It is under-inclusive because it is not recognised unconditionally to Union citizens, since there are Union citizens that may not exercise the rights connected with it.[20] It is over-inclusive because the personal scope of the freedom of movement includes individuals who do not have

EU citizenship. In fact, a number of third country nationals are covered by the *acquis* in relation to freedom of movement: Either because their stay is short;[21] or because of their personal situation or qualification (e.g. blue card, intracorporate transfers, long-term residents, researchers, students). It is therefore not entirely correct to call it an EU citizenship right, even though it is unquestionably an entitlement much appreciated by mobile Europeans.

Regardless of whether the rights of Union citizenship are to be understood as the legal entitlements the personal scope of which coincides with those having EU citizenship or if we are to take the label in a broader meaning, the point remains that these entitlements include rights of a very different nature (including liberties, powers, protections etc.) and type (civil, political, social, etc.); having different grounds (systematisation, mutual recognition, federal vocation, etc.) and being different in character (transnational, supranational, etc.) and scope (all nationals of member states, all residents, all having health insurance and not being threat to public safety, etc.). The political bottom-line of this set of entitlements is not different from any other set of rights. As Maas stressed a decade ago: 'as long as the resulting supranational citizenship continues to be based on a popular bargain among member states rather than enjoying widespread popular support, however, the rights of the common citizenship remain endangered in the same way that citizenship rights everywhere remain contingent upon continued support from leaders and publics' (Maas 2007, p. 6).

2.4   Conclusion

The Maastricht Treaty introduced a new status, that of the European citizen, in 1992. A person holds European citizenship if she is a national of a member state for the purposes of community law. Those who hold this status enjoy a number of rights.

Some rights are associated with Union citizenship even thought their personal scope of application does not coincide with those individuals who hold nationality of a member state, the *conditio sine qua non* of access to Union citizenship. Such rights include the right to petition Parliament and the Ombudsman, the right to access documents from European Parliament, Council and Commission and the right to good administration. It is important is to notice that the rights associated with Union citizenship include transnational rights like freedom of movement.

Freedom of movement is both over- and under-inclusive compared to the category of persons holding the nationality of a member state.

Other rights are more properly called 'citizens' rights' since they are only held by those who have the nationality of a member state. Such rights include political rights reserved for those having nationality of a member state, such as the right to vote and stand in election for second country nationals in local elections, the right to vote and stand in the elections of the European Parliament, and the right to adhere to a Citizens' initiative. These rights are called supranational because their purpose is to give political voice across borders.

The conclusion to draw from this swift overview of the entitlements connected with European citizenship is that the claim according to which having European citizenship or not has no impact on the rights one may hold is false. In the case of Brexit, exiting the Union means that all European citizens of British nationality risk losing rights associated with Union citizenship. Therefore it is misleading to claim that 'triggering Article 50 will not dilute or diminish anyone's statutory rights' (Tomkins 2016).

When first introduced, European citizenship was often depicted as being the world's first post-national status (Soysal 1994). It is connected to entitlements that may rightly be called supranational and transnational, but it is dependent on the nationality laws of European member states so therefore the characterisation using the prefix *post* might be a bit misleading. A better characterisation would be to say that European citizenship is a *status civitatis*, the criteria determining the access to and loss of which, are determined at the domestic level. It is also a *status sui generis*. It differs from nationality in unitary states and from dual citizenship in federal settings. Finally, it is connected to entitlements that are different in kind. We may call it a birth-right status in a multi-level polity. It is this status that some now fear losing. Next, let us try to understand what more precisely they fear.

NOTES

1. Bulletin of the European Communities, suppl. 5, 1975.
2. The common passport policy, which begun in the 1970s, is of considerable importance to what has been called 'the practice of citizenship' (streamlining practices for citizens of member states who reside in other member states). This policy aimed to enable the use of ID cards instead of passports within Community borders and equal treatment of nationals of member states by

third countries. The European Council approved the unifying passport policy at the Luxembourg Summit in 1979. In occasion of the Paris summit in 1974 and the Rome 1975 summit, the European Parliament pushed in this direction too. The delay in adopting the policy depended on the fact that passports fell into the exclusive competence of member states since it belonged to foreign policy.

3. See Bulletin of the European Communities, suppl. 7/75, *Towards the Europe of Citizens.*

4. See Bulletin of the European Communities, suppl. 1/1976, *European Union.*

5. The Treaty of Lisbon introduced, as known, a different numbering system so these articles are now to be found in the TFEU Art. 20–24. (ex Article 17 TEC), Article 21 (ex Article 18 TEC), Article 22 (ex Article 19 TEC), Article 23 (ex Article 20 TEC), Article 24 (ex Article 21 TEC).

6. See e.g. *Defrenne c. Sabena* (Case C-43/75 ECLI:EU:C:1976:56).

7. Here it is worth recalling that one of the first, if not the first, case brought before a court in which nationality was discussed concerned the UK: The case of the *post-nati* or *Calvin's case* opposed Edward Coke and Francis Bacon in 1608 on the issue of whether the founding of the UK had also led to the creation of a single *status civitatis*; if, that is, despite the diversity on the 'national' level, Scots and Englishmen were to be considered subjects with the same 'citizenship.' See Gough 1955; Wheeler 1947; Price 1997; Everson 2003; Cohen 2010.

8. It was not until January 1851 that Pasquale Stanislao Mancini, in his prolusion at the University in Turin, *Del principio di nazionalità come fondamento del diritto delle genti*, formulated the principle of nationality as the basis of authority relationship between the individual and state: The state becomes the institutional expression of the nation, providing the ideological reason for the Risorgimento movement in the unification of Italy. See Mindus 2014, Chapter 3.

9. Art. 5 states: 'Within a third State, a person having more than one nationality shall be treated as if he had only one. Without prejudice to the application of its law in matters of personal status and of any conventions in force, a third State shall, of the nationalities which any such person possesses, recognise exclusively in its territory either the nationality of the country in which he is habitually and principally resident, or the nationality of the country with which in the circumstances he appears to be in fact most closely connected.'

10. CIG *Nottebohm* (April 6, 1955) Liechtenstein v. Guatemala, full text available at http://www.icj-cij.org/docket/files/18/2674.pdf (last accessed 7 November 2016).

11. *Mario Vicente Micheletti v Delegación del Gobierno en Cantabria* (Case C-369/90).

12. See 1972 *Italian Project for a Convention Instituting a European Citizenship* [Progetto italiano per una convenzione istitutiva di una cittadinanza europea] in Sica 1979.

13. The ability to disconnect member state nationality from EU citizenship, although confirmed in *Kaur*, is much more difficult for the member states to use after *Rottmann*. See below and for more details Chapter 6.
14. *Protocol n. 2 to the Act of Accession, relating to the Faro Islands, art. 4, 1972* (OJ L 73 163).
15. See e.g. *Baubast* (C-413/99), *Martínez-Sala* (C-85/96), *Grzelczyk* (C-184/99), *Garcia Avello* (C-148/02) and *Bidar* (C-209/03).
16. Case C-135/08 *Janko Rottmann v Freistaat Bayern* [2010] ECR nyp, § 42.
17. C-300/4, *Eman and Sevinger*, EU:C:2006:545 [2006] ECRI-8055.
18. See e.g. Case C-503/09, *Lucy Stewart* EU:C:2011:500.
19. See e.g. Case C-224/02, *Pusa* (Opinion of A.G. Jacobs) EU:C:2003:634; Case C-406/04, *De Cuyper* EU:C:2006:491). For an analysis of these, see Strumia 2013.
20. See Case C-333/13 *Dano* EU:C:2014:2358.
21. Third country nationals holding a valid residence permit or visa have the right to move freely within the Schengen area for up to three months within a six-month period.

References

Bar-Yaacov, N. (1961) *Dual Nationality*, London: Stevens.

Bastide, S. (1956) 'L'affaire Nottebohm devant la Cour Internationale de Justice', 45 *Revue critique de droit international privé* 607–633.

Borras Rodriguez, A. (1993) 'Comment on the Micheletti Decision of the ECJ', 92 *Revista juridica de Catalunya*, 584–587.

Carrascosa, J. (1994) 'Dual Nationality and Community Law: The Micheletti Case', 1 *Tolleys Immigration and Nationality Law and Practice* 7–12.

Carrera Nunez, S., De Groot, G.-R. (eds.) (2015) *European Citizenship at the Crossroads. The Role of the European Union on Loss and Acquisition of Nationality*, Oisterwijk: Wolf.

Cohen, E.F. (2010) 'Jus Tempus in the Magna Carta: The Sovereignty of Time in Modern Politics and Citizenship', 43 *Political Science and Politics* 3, 463–466.

Cordini, G. (2003) 'La cittadinanza europea. Profili di diritto costituzionale comunitario e comparato', 1 *Il Politico* 73.

De Groot, R.-G. (2004) 'Towards a European Nationality Law' in 8 *Electronic Journal of Comparative Law*, available at: http://www.ejcl.org/83/art83-4.html (last accessed 20 January 2017).

Evans, A.C. (1991) 'Nationality Law and European Integration', 16 *European Law Review* 190ff.

Everson, M. (2003) 'Subjects or Citizens of Erewhon?', 7 *Citizenship Studies* 1, 65–83.

Garot, M.J. (1999) *La citoyenneté de l'Union européenne*, Paris: L'Harmattan.

Geogiadou, Z. (2015) 'Foreword', in S. Carrera Nunez, G.-R. De Groot (eds.) *European Citizenship at the Crossroads. The Role of the European Union on Loss and Acquisition of Citizenship* (ILEC), Oisterwijk: Wolf Legal Publishers.

Glazer, J.H. (1956) 'Affaire Nottebohm (Lichtenstein v. Guatemala), A Critique', 44 *Georgetown Law Journal* 313–325.

Gough, J.W. (1955) *Fundamental Law in English Constitutional History*, Oxford: Clarendon.

Hansen, R. (2002) *Dual Nationality, Social Rights and Federal Citizenship in the U.S. and Europe: The Reinvention of Citizenship*, New York: Berghahn Books.

Iglesias Buhigues, J.L. (1993) 'Doble nacionalidad y derecho comunitario. A propósito del asunto C 369/90, Micheletti', in M. Perez Gonzalez (ed.) *Hacia un nuovo orden international y europeo. Homenaje al prof. M. Diéz de Velasco*, Madrid: Tecnos, 953–967.

Jacobs, F.G. (1976) *The European Law and the Individual*, Amsterdam/New York: Elsevier.

Janis, M.W. (1984) 'Individuals as Subjects of International Law', 61 *Cornell International Law Journal* 61ff.

Jessurun d'Oliveira, H.U. (1993) 'Case-Note (Case C-369/90) M.V. Micheletti', 30 *Common Market Law Review* 623–637.

Kotalakidis, N. (2000) *Von der nationalen Staatsangehörigkeit zur Unionsbürgerschaft. Die Person und das Gemeinwesen*, Baden-Baden: Nomos.

Lippolis, V. (1994) *La cittadinanza europea*, Bologna: Il Mulino.

Maas, W. (2007) *Creating European Citizens*, Lanham: Rowman & Littlefield.

Marquand, D. (1979) *A Parliament for Europe*, London: Cape.

Marshall, T.H. (1950) *Citizenship and Social Class and Other Essays*, Cambridge: CUP.

Maury, J. (1958) 'L'arrêt Nottebohm et la condition de nationalité effective', 23 *Zeitschrift für ausländisches und internationales Privatrecht* 515–534.

Mindus, P. (2014) *Cittadini e no. Forme e funzioni dell'inclusione e dell'esclusione*, Florence: Firenze University Press.

Mindus, P., Goldoni, M. (2012) 'Between Democracy and Nationality: Citizenship Policies in the Lisbon Ruling', 18 *European Public Law* 2, 351–371.

Nascimbene, B. (1986) 'Nationality Law and Citizenship', in B. Nascimbene (ed.) *Nationality Laws in the European Union*, London: Butterworths.

Nascimbene, B. (1998) 'Towards a European Law on Citizenship and Nationality?', in S. O'Leary (ed.) *Citizenship and Nationality Status in New Europe*, London: Sweet & Maxwell.

Price, P.J. (1997) 'Natural Law and Birthright Citizenship in Calvin's Case', 9 *Yale Journal of Law and the Humanities* 1, Winter.

Quadri, R. (1936) *La sudditanza nel diritto internazionale*, Padova: Cedam.

Ruzié, D. (1993) 'Nationalité, effectivité en droit communautaire', 97 *Revue générale de droit international public* 107–120.

Sabourin, N. (1999) *The Relevance of the European Convention on Nationality for Non-European States* in *1st European Conference on Nationality: Trends and Developments in National and International Law on Nationality*, Council of Europe, 18 and 19 October *1999*, available at http://www.coe.int/t/dghl/standardsetting/nationality/Conference%201%20(1999)Proceedings.pdf (last accessed 7 November 2016)

Schade, H. (1995) 'The Draft European Convention on Nationality', 49 *Austrian Journal of Public and International Law* 2, 99–103.

Schönberger, C. (2005) *Unionsbürger: Europas föderales Bürgerrecht in vergleichender Sicht*, Tübingen: Mohr.

Sébastien, G. (1993) 'La citoyenneté de l'Union européenne', 5 *Revue de droit public et de la science politique en France et à l'étranger* 1267.

Sica, M. (ed.) (1979) *Verso la cittadinanza europea*, Firenze: Le Monnier.

Soysal, Y. (1994) *Limits of Citizenship. Migrants and Postnational Membership in Europe*, Chicago: Chicago University Press.

Strumia, F. (2013) 'Looking for Substance at the Boundaries: European Citizenship and Mutual Recognition of Belonging', 32 *Yearbook of European Law* 432–459.

Tomkins, A. (2016) 'Brexit, Democracy and the Rule of Law', *VerfBlog*, 2016/11/06 available at http://verfassungsblog.de/brexit-democracy-and-the-rule-of-law/ (last accessed 7 November 2016).

Trevisani, M.P. (1995) *I soggetti dell'Unione Europea*, Padova: Cedam.

Vanel, M. (1951) 'La notion de nationalité. Évolution historique en droit interne et en droit colonial comparé', *Revue critique de droit international privé*, 40.

Weis, P. (1979) *Nationality and Statelessness in International Law*, 2nd ed., London: Stevens & Sons.

Wheeler, H. (1947) *Calvin's Case and the Empire*, (Ph.D. diss.), Indiana University.

CHAPTER 3

A Sudden Loss of Rights

Abstract This chapter presents the problem of legal uncertainty afflicting second country nationals in the UK and British citizens turning from expats to post-European third country nationals. First we look at the case of European citizens living in the UK and then we look at British citizens residing in other parts of the Union. Real-world cases are presented. The narration of the cases enables the reader to appreciate the multitude of effects and the layers of issues involved. They also allow pointing out how dramatic a change like Brexit may be in the lives of those involved. The reader who feels comfortable in mastering the legal complexities affecting those who have relied on free movement in making their life choices can move on to the next chapter.

Keywords European citizenship · Brexit · Second country national · Third country national · United Kingdom · Freedom of movement · Right of residence · EU law · Migration law

There is a lot of uncertainty about the future situation of second country nationals in the UK and of British nationals in other parts of the EU. There are political reasons for fearing that second country nationals after Brexit may face a 'dramatic loss of rights' (Kochenov 2016a). To some, this is 'one of the most serious risks of a UK withdrawal from the EU' (Douglas-Scott 2016). As evidenced by Jo Shaw, 'UK have long been

© The Author(s) 2017
P. Mindus, *European Citizenship after Brexit*, Palgrave Studies in European Union Politics, DOI 10.1007/978-3-319-51774-2_3

uncomfortable navigating the space between the political truth of popular hostility to immigration and the legal commitments of the UK to the EU Treaties. On that account, EU citizens exercising free movement rights are simply "lucky immigrants"' (Shaw 2016).[1] It has been submitted that 'to abolish many of these rights *en bloc*, with minimal or no parliamentary scrutiny, undermines fundamental rights, but is also undemocratic and detrimental to the parliamentary sovereignty' (Douglas-Scott 2015).

In the event of a non-negotiated exit, Union citizens would lose their right to live in the UK based on the Treaties and EEA nationals in the UK will no longer benefit from the rights contained in the *Citizens Directive* 2004/38/EC, implemented into British domestic law via the Immigration (EEA) Regulations from 2006. The UK could apply its national immigration laws to all EEA citizens, that would require (merely) repealing s 7(1) of the Immigration Act 1988, which provides that leave to enter or remain in the UK under the Immigration Act 1971 is not required by a person who is entitled to enter the UK by virtue of EU rights.

Any arrangements that allow EU citizens to continue to live and work in the UK have to be negotiated, just as UK nationals in member states who will lose Union citizenship after EU law ceases to include them in its 'personal sphere of validity' (Kelsen 1945). Also prospective EU migrants, that is, those who wish to migrate to the UK after Brexit would be affected, but I shall leave this aside.[2] They would be subjected to the full force of British immigration law in the event of an agreement-less exit, but in absence of 'acquired rights.' An intriguing case would be family members wishing to join second country nationals in the UK: Can they claim rights if the family relationship is prior to Brexit? Most certainly, they would be excluded from the protection offered within the ambit of Union law: The ECJ has qualified the 'genuine substance' doctrine of *Ruiz Zambrano* pointing out that the mere desire to keep a family together does not constitute ground for accommodating claims by third country nationals.[3]

Naturally, the so-called vested rights for EU citizens in the UK and for UK citizens in the EU cover a much broader subject matter than freedom of movement, including, for example, social policy, non-discrimination law and fundamental rights. Here we will deal foremost with free movement since the Brexit debate centred on migration. Even narrowing down the topic in this way the numerous difficulties that emerge promise an increased workload ahead.

Modifications in legal position will affect approx. 2.9 million non-British EU citizens in the UK and approx. 690,000 UK citizens currently living in EU member states. This assertion stands in stark contrast to often repeated claims: The media has reported that second country nationals in the UK would amount to 3–3.3 million and that UK citizens residing in other member states would amount to 1.2–1.3 million. A few sources refer to the unofficial data of the Migration Observatory based on its analysis of Labour Force Survey.[4] But most sources take these figures from the UN.[5] This data, however, refers to persons residing in a country or geographical area by their *country of birth*. Legal positions are not held in virtue of 'place of birth' but citizenship: *Ius soli* at birth is not the sole mode of acquisition of nationality. *Ius sanguinis* allows for naturalisation abroad and acquisition of nationality by birth for persons born abroad. EU citizenship depends on the *nationality* of a member state, pursuant to Art. 20(1) TFEU. Eurostat records nationality, making it a preferable source of data. 'The use of UN data in this context may result in discrepancies and misrepresentation of the impact of Brexit of UK and EU nationals' (Carrera et al. 2016). Not even Eurostat data is to be relied upon entirely: National statistics may include dual nationals holding UK and the reporting country's nationality. Eurostat data is nonetheless preferable to UN data. Based on Eurostat data combined with the UK Office for National Statistics (ONS), there were around 2.9 million second country nationals residing in the UK on 1 January 2015. Polish, Irish and Romanian nationals are top three of second country nationalities present in the UK. There were also around 690,000 British citizens residing in other EU member states.[6] The majority of these UK citizens reside in Spain, but a significant number are living in Ireland, Germany, the Netherlands, Italy, Belgium and Sweden.

Behind the numbers, there are individuals who, according to their specific circumstances, will be affected by Brexit in quite different ways. Let us start by looking more closely, in the next section, at the situation for second country nationals living in the UK and then, in Section 3.2, at the situation of British nationals residing in other parts of the Union. The narration of the real-world cases presented below aim to enable appreciation of the multitude of effects and the layers of issues involved. They also allow pointing out how dramatic a change like Brexit may be in the lives of those involved. The reader who feels comfortable in mastering the legal complexities affecting those who have relied on free movement in making their life choices can move on to the next chapter.

3.1   THE HOME OFFICE'S NEW WORKLOAD

Second country nationals in the UK will not lose their status as Union citizens; they recover full rights on return to the 'territory of the Union' (Azoulai 2014) and keep non-territorial rights associated with European citizenship, such as consular protection. It is not evident either that EU citizens resident in the UK will automatically be subjected to restricted political rights because of Brexit. Twenty-two member states allow their citizens to vote for the European Parliament when they reside in a non-EU state.[7] Additionally:

> there are sound reasons for the EU institutions to pressure the remaining five to change their policy, especially in light of the Court of Justice's *Zambrano* ratio that Member States should not hinder 'the genuine enjoyment of the substance of rights conferred by virtue of their status as citizens of the Union'. Moreover, it is not implausible that the Court of Justice's *Delvigne* will prompt a legal challenge to disenfranchisement of Union citizens residing in non-EU Member States (Ziegler 2016).

Given that Article 20 TFEU does not make any reference to residence, the scope of personal validity of European citizenship cannot be limited with reference to residence, as shown in *Eman & Sevinger*.[8] For European migrants in the UK – simply 'aliens' after Brexit – the withdrawal agreement is key to understanding their future situation. According to an often-made statement – to be tested – those with permanent residence would be given indefinite leave to remain.[9] But a number of hard cases are susceptible of arising. In particular, there is a timing problem for defining 'acquired rights': Will the negotiated solution take into consideration rights in the process of being acquired such as legal positions of those who are working towards a permanent right of residence? Or will there be a cut off date for determining acquired rights? Will that date be Brexit? Will all those who had not matured the permanent right to reside by Brexit-day have their right to stay invalidated *ex tunc*?

Consider, for example, Charlotte, the 15-year-old daughter of French citizens living in London: Will she have a claim to equal treatment in respect of university fees as she will turn 18 after Brexit date? And will a degree taken in the UK even be recognised in EU27?[10] Or take Belgian Olivier, a self-employed psychologist in Bristol, who gets married to his girlfriend from Singapore: Will he be able to bring his spouse to the UK or will he need to prove, in accordance with the more restrictive British policy, that he earns £18,600 pa, which he, as almost half of the UK population, does not? The Greek Stephanos worked a couple of years on a part-time low paying teaching job before obtaining a PhD grant. Students also need to have a 'comprehensive sickness insurance' but he is among the 1/1000 inhabitants in Europe with a diagnosis of multiple scleroses, so no private insurer will insure him for 'previously existing conditions.' Will he lose the right to reside that he was in the process of acquiring or can he retain his previous worker condition? This also puzzles Leila from Luxembourg who did have a job, but that she was forced to leave while pregnant. As primary carer of her two-year-old son David, she has not yet found employment. Will she be able to stay? Sean is sarcastic and thinks the very existence of multiple citizenship undermines the point of Brexit, if the point was – as Cameron has stated – an issue about immigration. In a pub in Belfast he argues that dual citizenship may be the answer for many. That European citizens are naturalising in the UK (or at least seeking permanent residence documentation as the first step to naturalisation) would be an indication of how to stay as a UK citizen while keeping EU citizenship. This prospect seems less convincing to Robert from Vienna who fears that the ban on multiple nationality enforced in certain member states, makes it rather implausible.

Furthermore, consider the Italian Irene who has been part-time student and part-time waitress in the City for eight years and is married to Andrea, from Brazil, who got in on a visa as a family member of a European citizen in 2014 and still has three years left on visa when Brexit occurs: Irene finds out that she can naturalise but if she does, Andrea might lose the ability to exercise treaty rights in the UK.[11] Irene figures that the UK will still be bound by the *European Convention of Human Rights* (ECHR): Its Article 8 on 'family life' is widely drawn and the case-law – she is told by a friend who studied law – has proven that Art. 8 would cover Andrea's 'legitimate expectation to live in the country.' But if she is wrong, Andrea might need to leave for Brazil. Should Irene apply for naturalisation?

Now, consider self-sufficient Ulrike from Germany, who has been married to Peter, and living in Sussex for almost two decades. She now discovers that, for the Home Office, her ability to use the NHS – which she has regularly used most notably when giving birth to their children – does not count as 'comprehensive sickness insurance' so therefore she has never built up a right of residence.[12] She was just physically present in the UK, they tell her. But she knows she could get a European health insurance card from her home country and even get it backdated. There is a reciprocal healthcare arrangement with Germany. The Home Office, though, requires her to sign a declaration if she wants to use for this option: She must declare that she has no intention of staying permanently in the UK: What is she going to tell her husband?

More worried, however, is Francisca from Lisbon, who came to England a decade ago, at the age of eight with her abusive father who found a job in a manufacturing in Herefordshire. Her younger brother Santiago, aged 17, who always seems to get into trouble, has been sentenced to deportation after committing a crime in the UK punishable with imprisonment for 12 months. Prior to Brexit, European citizens could be removed only on serious grounds of public policy and public security, pursuant to Art. 28 of the 2004 *Citizens Directive*. But after Brexit, the law that applies might be Section 3(5) IA 1971 of the domestic legal order that commands at the second comma (b) to deport a non-UK citizen if 'another person to whose family he belongs is or has been ordered to be deported.' Even though pregnant and a long-term resident of the UK, Francisca fears she might be expelled since Brexit Britain would not need to comply with the European law principle of proportionality that has hitherto mitigated removal practices. Post-Brexit UK could thus practice removals without paying due attention to age, health status, family or economic situation, social and cultural integration into the host society. Notable in this perspective are also the key provisions for automatic deportation of non EEA-nationals under UK *Border Act* 2007. Is her fear misplaced? Can the UK pursue an energetic expulsion policy?

Legal uncertainty is destined to increase. It may be relevant to address the hard cases to come in a future Brexit withdrawal treaty and/or treaties over the future relations with the UK so as to curb future litigation and limit the number of administrative errors that are likely to rise, given 'the manifest inability of the Home Office and the various associated agencies even to deal effectively with their existing workload without putting several million more people under immigration control' (Shaw 2016).

3.2   FROM EXPAT TO POST-EUROPEAN

No matter the shape, Brexit would impact significantly on the citizenship of the Union, in a particularly unhappy way for British nationals living in the Union. The citizenry is predicted to shrink in size, change in composition and some parts of it will be left in potentially vulnerable positions.

The Union citizenry has of course always been dynamic, not merely due to inherent demographical factors and enlargement but also due to modifications of member states' nationality laws. To give examples pertinent to the UK, there was an artificial increase of the number of British nationals when the status was extended to include the inhabitants of the Falklands in 1983, the population of Hong Kong in 1997 and to some 200,000 *citizens of British overseas territories* in 2002 (De Groot 2004, p. 7).[13] Brexit, however, constitutes a novelty: For the first time we are witnessing an automatic and collective lapse of status for Union citizens of exclusively British nationality.

Brexit is expected to cause an automatic *en masse* loss of European citizenship for individuals, residing on both sides of the border of the UK. Particularly vulnerable are those who have relied on free movement in making their life choices. Unsurprisingly, anecdotal evidence from Belgium has suggested large numbers of British residents there making applications for citizenship. The media has reported that across 18 European member states, some 2,800 Britons applied for citizenship in the first eight months of 2016, estimated to correspond to a more than 250% increase on numbers recorded in 2015.[14]

A non-negotiated Brexit would transform all Union citizens of exclusively British nationality in *third country nationals* (TCNs): They would lose rights associated with the status, including freedom of movement and residence,[15] voting rights in municipal[16] and European Parliament elections, consular protection by another EU country, right to adhere to European citizens' initiatives (Art. 11 TEU & Art. 24 TFEU) as well as the principle that holds EU citizenship rights together, that is, the right to non-discrimination on grounds of nationality (Art. 18 TFEU) – viewed by some as the groundbreaking thrust of Union citizenship (Kostakopoulou 2008; Eleftheriadis 2012) and by others as a normatively suspect way of clinging to market citizenship (Somek 2011). Along with the status goes also jurisprudentially developed protections, such as the right to export benefits and entitlements tied to nationality in a host member state[17] and the right not to be burdened, or discriminated for having exercised the freedom to move.[18]

Not all British citizens would lose rights associated with European citizenship whose personal scope is over-inclusive in respect of having the nationality in a member state. British citizens in the Union would retain these rights also as third country nationals. These rights are often called 'citizens' rights' but they are really recognised to all residents: Such as the right to petition Parliament and the Ombudsman (Article 24) from the Maastricht Treaty, the right, introduced with the Nice Charter in 2000, to access documents from European Parliament, Council and Commission (Art. 42) and the right to good administration (Art. 41). Neither would UK nationals lose the right, introduced with the Treaty of Amsterdam in 1997, to address the EU in any official language and to receive a reply in that same language (Art. 24), since other member states use English as official language.

Moreover, the EU has partially harmonised immigration laws: Article 77 TFEU provides that the Union is competent to adopt rules relating to the absence of internal border controls, the management of external borders and short stay visa policy; Article 79 TFEU provides that the Union may adopt rules relating to the conditions of entry and residence, the definition of the rights of third country nationals residing legally, illegal immigration and unauthorised residence and combating human trafficking. Harmonisation in these areas means that the laws applicable to British citizens in the Union would be a mixture of common European standards and the residual domestic immigration laws of each of the member states. Basically, it entails increased scrutiny of British nationals at EU borders.

The Union could impose visa requirements, including for short-term trips and holidays, since the UK is not a party to the earlier treaty on *Regulations governing the Movement of Persons between Member States* of the Council of Europe from 1957 that abolished visa requirements between European states. Steve Peers, for one, argues that visas might be imposed on all EU travel after a Brexit (Peers 2016b). He has also argued that:

> the EU would be free to impose visa requirements on UK citizens in the event of withdrawal. While the EU tends not to impose visa requirements on wealthy countries, it does expect such countries (such as the USA and Canada) in return to exempt all EU citizens from a visa. So if the UK wished to impose visas (for instance) on Romanians and Bulgarians, it would face pressure from the EU to waive such requirements – or face the imposition of a visa requirement for UK citizens (Peers 2016a).

Those who sought to reside for longer periods in the Union would be subject to the EU rules on immigration including quotas and EU-preference rules on labour migration. 'The transition from freedom to restriction will be painful for many. There will be many cases that fall through the cracks, and vast amounts of insecurity and pain' (Shaw 2016).

Consider, for example, Timothy who is a ballet dancer in Paris. Would he be granted a Blue Card to continue the profession or would he be considered self-employed subjected to the intricate French regulations? How about his flatmate Christopher who works as an assistant on a project at a local university: Does he now fall within the remit of the European Directive on third country national researchers?[19] What happens to Margaret, who is one of the 106,610 claiming UK pension in Spain?[20] She sold her house in Cambridgeshire and retired on the Costa Brava. Will the European rules that guarantee the upgrading of her British pension no longer apply? Sally, an unpaid trainee at a multinational in Amsterdam, is offered work in a subsidiary in Slovakia: Can she accept and bring her husband with her? Would she discover she needed to fall within the remit of the intra-corporate transfers? Or within the remit of the European Directive on Students?[21] How about Ryan who catwalks for the autumn collection in Milan: Would he have some limited equality rights under the *single permit directive* (2011/98/EU) or would he be considered a seasonal worker, in which case his residence would be subject to a strict time limit?[22] Bryce, who teaches English in Krakow, will have a tough time bringing over his mother Allie who needs care: She would count as third country national family member and member states have stricter domestic regulations on family reunion than the regime applicable to Union citizens. Cillian, originally from Belfast, has been living in Madrid for over a decade working as a software developer. Frustrated by not having his say in the referendum, he considers naturalising to fool his country's intention of stripping him of his rights as European citizen. Would he be able to pass the language proficiency test (DELE, Diplomas de Español como Lengua Extranjera) and another one on his knowledge of Spain (CCSE, La prueba de conocimientos constitucionales y socioculturales de España) that Spain imposes since October 2015? Would he need to renounce his original nationality to naturalise in Spain? Kylie, from Gibraltar, runs a bed and breakfast in Barcelona since 2010: Will she be required to apply for the European status of long-term residency for third country nationals or can she keep the more advantageous permanent residency? Dexter is part of an avant-garde theatre group in Amsterdam but he lacks any serious command of Dutch: Can he naturalise or will he be hindered by the 'integration test' the Netherlands imposes since 2007? Abigail, who is a part-time tourist guide in Stockholm, is anxious about her studies in biology: Would they let her continue working? Will she now need to pay the 15,000-euro tuition fees for non-EU nationals?

Annabel came to Rome as a student. She has a relationship with an older, married man and does not want to go home. Her American cousin over-stayed her visa in Australia. Can she just stay put? Maybe her lover will file for divorce? Maybe not. If she stays put, can she be detained? According to the EU's *Return Directive* (2008/115/EC), post-Brexit British citizens who do not, or no longer, have a right to stay would have to be expelled, by force if they did not go voluntarily. To facilitate departure, they could be detained for up to six months, or up to 18 months if there were complications with their removal.

While UK citizenship is currently seen as part of the elite club of the top-quality nationalities scholars predict a drastic fall in value. Dimitry Kochenov speaks of 'one of the most radical losses in the value of a particular nationality in recent history (...) a loss of 30% of UK nation-ality's value, an overwhelming downgrade to the level of Argentinian and Chilean nationality' (Kochenov 2016a).[23] This effect is partially due to the fact that entitlements tied to national citizenship are, albeit with many caveats, made exportable, which basically extends the reach of national citizenship across its national borders: There is differential treatment between claims made against host member states and those made against home member states. Claims against host states are subjected to stricter conditions (e.g. Case C-308/14 *Commission v United Kingdom*; Case C-333/13 *Dano*) whereas claims against home states to looser conditions (e.g. Case C-359/13 *Martens*). This has led to the claim that Union citizenship would rather reinforce national citizenship, than the opposite (Strumia 2015; *contra* Davies 2005).

An agreementless Brexit, some claim, means 'that UK citizens in the EU would have a legal position inferior to Russians and Moroccans (whose countries have non-discrimination agreements with the EU)' (Kochenov 2016b).[24] For some, 'British expatriates in the EU will be, in effect, the eggs that have to be broken to make the omelets of those British politicians who feel uncomfortable living next to Romanians' (Peers 2014).

The tales of Oliver, Francisca, Ryan, Abigail and the others work as a powerful reminder of the fact that people all around the Union rely on their treaty rights to make life choices. It is not only libraries – *pace* von Kirchmann – that 'only three words of the legislature can destroy.' Let us see if we are able to give some solace to them. I suggest doing so requires advancing a theoretically informed inquiry. But first let us be clear about why such a take is needed.

NOTES

1. The reported surge in hate-crimes registered post-Brexit seems to confirm the reading.
2. For a broader impact assessment, see Peers 2016a.
3. See Joint Cases 356/11 and 357/11, *O, S* EU:C:2012:776, § 52; Case C-87/12, *Ymeraga* EU:C:2013:291, § 38. Also see Case C-86/12, *Alokpa* EU:C:2013:645.
4. See http://www.migrationobservatory.ox.ac.uk/resources/commentaries/ today-gone-tomorrow-status-eu-citizens-already-living-uk/ (last accessed 12 November 2016).
5. UN DESA Population Division (2015), 'Trends in international migrant stock: the 2015 Revision,' UN. Doc. POP/DB/MIG/Stock/Rev.2015.
6. See Eurostat (2016), 'Population on 1 January by five year age group, sex and citizenship (migr_pop1ctz)' (http://ec.europa.eu/eurostat/web/population-demography-migration-projections/population-data/database/).
7. EU Parliament report, Disenfranchisement of EU citizens resident abroad, June 2015, available at http://www.europarl.europa.eu/RegData/etudes/ IDAN/2015/564379/EPRS_IDA(2015)564379_EN.pdf (last accessed 12 November 2016).
8. Non-discrimination on the grounds of nationality, the very principle holding together the legal positions attributed to Union citizens, applies independently of residence on 'Union territory' (C-300/4, *Eman and Sevinger*, EU:C:2006:545 [2006] ECRI-8055].
9. The Leave campaigned made this claim: http://www.voteleavetakecontrol. org/restoring_public_trust_in_immigration_policy_a_points_based_non_ discriminatory_immigration_system. A 2016 lib-dem bill advocates a 'sunset clause' that would allow EU citizens to continue on the track of acquiring right of permanent residence or indefinite leave to remain for a number of coming years. Indefinite leave offers fewer protections against deportation than permanent residence. In general, a leave is a concession and not a right. The Belgian *Cour Constitutionnelle* has formulated the point in crystal clear terms: the grant of a residence permit '*constitue une faveur et non un droit*' (*Cour Constitutionnelle*, judgment of 26 September 2013, no. 123, available at http://www.const-court.be/public/f/2013/2013-123f.pdf, at 7).
10. Scholars have also pointed out the risk of 'brain drain' from the UK: Shaw 2016.
11. The fact that naturalising involves loss of Treaty rights is entrenched in the EU citizenship idea. Notice that the history of EU citizenship is strongly marked in this sense: already at the Paris summit 1977 when talk of 'European identity' pushed for the acknowledgement of 'special rights' (i.e. privileges) for nationals of member states in respect of nationals of

non-member states, the Report presented by the Commission to the Council on 3 July 1975, Commission of EC, Bulletin of the European Communities, Supplement 5/75, COM (75) 321 final, Brussels 2 July 1975, stated at 32: 'in the view of the probable development of the Community this possibility [of encouraging the naturalisation of workers going to other member states] involving a simple exchange of nationality seems less promising than the idea of equality with the nationals of the host State.' On the history of EU citizenship see Maas 2007.

12. According to barrister Colin Yeo, there are tens of thousands of persons in this situation. Watch Migrants' Rights Network, Q&A on EU migrants rights after Brexit, available at https://www.youtube.com/watch?v= Doi3KYfkbp8&spfreload=5 (last accessed 30 October 2016). Generally on the situation of Germans in the UK, Mulder 2016.

13. On the 'fabrication of citizens' and its political consequences, see Mindus 2014, chapter 3 section 6. On the multiplicity of statuses in British nationality law see Sawyer and Wray 2014.

14. See https://www.theguardian.com/politics/2016/oct/19/huge-increase-britons-seeking-citizenship-eu-states-brexit-looms (last accessed 30 October 2016).

15. Freedom of movement and residence is not an entitlement strictly linked to Union citizenship: its *ratio personae* is both over- and under-inclusive. It is not recognised unconditionally to Union citizens (as underscored by Case C-333/13 *Dano* EU:C:2014:2358) and a number of third country nationals are covered by *acquis* in relation to freedom of movement. Third country nationals holding a valid residence permit or visa have the right to move freely within the Schengen area for up to three months within a six-month period, the rights in relation to taking up residence for a period exceeding three months in another member state is covered by specific legal instruments, depending on their status, and subject to conditions in national legislation (e.g. blue card, intracorporate transfers, long-term residents, researchers, students). See Spaventa 2008; García Andrade 2014, 111 ff.

16. Except the 12 member states were provided for by national law. See the seminal comparative work in Shaw 2007.

17. See e.g. Case C-503/09, *Lucy Stewart* EU:C:2011:500.

18. See e.g. Case C-224/02, *Pusa* (Opinion of A.G. Jacobs) EU:C:2003:634; Case C-406/04, *De Cuyper* EU:C:2006:491). For an analysis of these, see Strumia 2013, pp. 441–447.

19. EU Directive on third country national researchers 2005/71 EC, 12/10/ 2005 OJ L 289, 18.6.2009, 17–29.

20. Data from Department for Work and Pensions: http://tabulation-tool.dwp. gov.uk/100pc/sp/cccountry/cat/ccgor/a_carate_r_cccountry_c_cat_p_ ccgor_claimants_living_abroad_aug15.html (last accessed 30 October 2016).

21. Directive 2004/114/EC on the conditions of admission of TCN for the purposes of studies, pupil exchange, unremunerated training or voluntary service. See also De Witte 2013.
22. See the Directive 2014/36/EU of the European Parliament and of the Council of 26 February 2014 on the conditions of entry and stay of third-country nationals for the purpose of employment as seasonal workers.
23. Contrarily to Viviane Reding, according to whom 'one should not put a price tag on Union citizenship' (Speech before European Commission 'European citizenship should not be up for sale,' Speech/14/18, 15 January 2014), this is being done: See the newly launched index of the 'value' of nationality quality of nationality index that was developed by Kochenov in collaboration with Henley & Partners: see https://www.natio nalityindex.com/ (last accessed 30 October 2016). It is being used by governments to see how valuable their citizenship is, by prospective buyers to check the merchandise, and by those making projections on the 'value' of citizenship.
24. The number of applications to the Maltese individual investor program that have been withdrawn after the referendum is telling.

References

Azoulai, L. (2014) 'The (Mis)Construction of the European Individual. Two Essays on Union Citizenship Law', EUI Working Paper LAW 2014/14.
Carrera, S., Guild, E., Chun Luk, N. (2016) 'What Does Brexit Mean for the EU's Area of Freedom, Security and Justice?,' CEPS, July 2016, available at https://www.ceps.eu/publications/what-does-brexit-mean-eu%E2%80%99s-area-free dom-security-and-justice (last accessed 30 October 2016).
Davies, G. (2005) '"Any Place I Hang My Hat" or Residence is the New Nationality', 11 Environmental Law Journal 43.
De Groot, G.R. (2004) 'Towards a European Nationality Law', 8 Electronic Journal of Comparative Law, available at http://www.ejcl.org/83/art83-4.html (last accessed 30 October 2016).
De Witte, F. (2013) 'Who Funds the Mobile Student? Shedding Some Light on the Normative Assumptions Underlying EU Free Movement Law', 50 Common Market Law Review 203.
Douglas-Scott, S. (2015) 'Constitutional Implications of a UK Exit from the EU: Some Questions that Really Must be Asked', U.K. Const. L. Blog, (17th Apr 2015), available at https://ukconstitutionallaw.org/2015/04/17/sionaidh-douglas-scott-constitutional-implications-of-a-uk-exit-from-the-eu-some-ques tions-that-really-must-be-asked/ (last accessed 30 October 2016).

Douglas-Scott, S. (2016) 'What Happens to Acquired Rights in the Event of Brexit?', U.K. Const. L. Blog (16th May 2016), available at https://ukconsti tutionallaw.org/2016/05/16/sionaidh-douglas-scott-what-happens-to-acquired-rights-in-the-event-of-a-brexit/ (last accessed 30 October 2016).

Eleftheriadis, P. (2012) 'Citizenship and Obligation', in J. Dickson, P. Eleftheriadis (eds.) *Philosophical Foundations of European Union Law*, Oxford: OUP.

Eurostat. (2016) 'Population on 1 January by five year age group, sex and citizenship (migr_pop1ctz)', available at http://appsso.eurostat.ec.europa.eu/nui/show.do?dataset=migr_pop1ctz&lang=en (last accessed 20 January 2017).

García Andrade, P. (2014) 'Priviledged Third-Country Nationals and Their Right to Free Movement and Residence to and in the EU: Questions of Status and Competence', in E. Guild, C. Gortázar Rotaeche, D. Kostakopoulou (eds.) *The Reconceptualization of European Union Citizenship*, Leiden: Brill, 111 ff.

Kelsen, H. (1945) *General Theory of Law and State*, Cambridge, MA: Harvard University Press.

Kochenov, D. (2016) [2016a] *EU Citizenship and Withdrawals from the Union: How Inevitable is the Radical Downgrading of Rights?*, LEQS Paper No. 111/2016, available at http://www.lse.ac.uk/europeanInstitute/LEQS%20Discussion% 20Paper%20Series/LEQSPaper111.pdf (last accessed 30 October 2016).

Kochenov, D. (2016) [2016b] 'Brexit and the Argentinianisation of British Citizenship: Taking Care Not to Overstay Your 90 Days in Rome, Amsterdam or Paris', *VerfBlog*, 2016/6/24, available at http://verfassungsblog.de/brexit-and-the-argentinisation-of-british-citizenship-taking-care-not-to-overstay-your-90-days-in-rome-amsterdam-or-paris/ (last accessed 30 October 2016).

Kostakopoulou, D. (2008) *The Future Governance of Citizenship*, Cambridge: CUP.

Maas, W. (2007) *Creating European Citizens*, Lanham: Rowman & Littlefield Publishers.

Mindus, P. (2014) *Cittadini e no. Forme e funzioni dell'inclusione e dell'esclusione*, Florence: Firenze University Press.

Mulder, J. (2016) 'The Personal Implications of the Referendum Results for (German) EU Citizens Living in the UK', *German Law Journal – Brexit Supplement*, available at https://static1.squarespace.com/static/56330ad3e4b0733dcc0c8495/t/5776e5e6579fb3bc18d93eab/1467409894916/15+PDF_Vol_17_Brexit +_Mulder.pdf (last accessed 30 October 2016).

Peers, S. (2014) 'What Happens to British Expatriates?', Blog entry from 9 May 2014 EU Law Analysis Blog, available at http://eulawanalysis.blog spot.se/2014/05/what-happens-to-british-expatriates-if.html (last accessed 30 October 2016).

Peers, S. (2016) [2016a] 'Migration, Internal Security and the UK's EU Membership', 87 *The Political Quarterly* 2, 247–253, April–June 2016.

Peers, S. (2016) [2016b] 'Goodbye, Cruel World: Visas for Holidays After Brexit?', Blog entry from 25 April 2016 EU Law Analysis, available at http://eulawanalysis.blogspot.se/2016/04/goodbye-cruel-world-visas-for-holidays.html (last accessed 30 October 2016).

Sawyer, C., Wray, H. (2014) *EUDO Country Report: United Kingdom* (revised and updated 2014), available at http://cadmus.eui.eu/bitstream/handle/1814/33839/EUDO-CIT_2014_01_UK.pdf (last accessed 30 October 2016).

Shaw, J. (2007) *The Transformations of Citizenship in the European Union. Electoral Rights and Restructuration of Political Space,* Cambridge: CUP.

Shaw, J. (2016) 'Citizenship, Migration and Free Movement in Brexit Britain', 17 *German Law Journal – Brexit Special Supplement,* available at https://static1.squarespace.com/static/56330ad3e4b0733dcc0c8495/t/577ef48c20099e34c7327fe1/1467937934684/19+PDF_Vol_17_Brexit+_Shaw.2.pdf (last accessed 30 October 2016).

Somek, A. (2011) *Engineering Equality. An Essay on European Anti-Discrimination Law,* Oxford: OUP.

Spaventa, E. (2008) 'Seeing the Woods Despite the Trees? On the Scope of Union Citizenship and its Constitutional Effects', 45 *Common Market Law Review* 13.

Strumia, F. (2013) 'Looking for Substance at the Boundaries: European Citizenship and Mutual Recognition of Belonging', 32 *Yearbook of European Law* 432–459.

Strumia, F. (2015) 'The Asymmetry in the Right to Free Movement of European Union Citizens: The Case of Students', Blog entry from 12 May 2015 EU Law Analysis, available at http://eulawanalysis.blogspot.se/2015/07/the-asymmetry-in-right-to-free-movement.html (last accessed 30 October 2016).

Ziegler, R. (2016) 'The Referendum of the UK's EU Membership: No Legal Salve for its Disenfranchised Non-resident Citizens', *VerfBlog,* 21/06/2016, available at http://verfassungsblog.de/the-referendum-of-the-uks-eu-membership-no-legal-salve-for-its-disenfranchised-non-resident-citizens/ (last accessed 30 October 2016).

CHAPTER 4

Understanding Citizenship: The Functionalist Approach

Abstract This chapter starts by explaining why a theoretically informed inquiry is needed. Such an inquiry is warranted for a number of reasons that include political volatility, lack of relevant precedents and the fact that conventional approaches do not lead to many policy suggestions for solving the hard cases at hand. It is suggested that Brexit may place us before a constitutional dilemma: Can Article 50 be taken seriously without giving up rights? The functionalist theory that this study adopts is outlined and explained. Three ways in which it applies to Brexit are distinguished. These three directions of inquiry are developed in the rest of the book.

Keywords European citizenship · Functionalist theory of citizenship · Brexit · EU law

4.1 Four Arguments in Favour of Theory

A theoretically informed inquiry is needed, I submit, to understand European citizenship after Brexit. An explanation is needed on why we ought to abandon the more traditional or mainstream analysis of the issue that has hitherto prevailed both among scholars and in the media. There are a number of reasons for favouring a different approach. These include the political volatility surrounding the matter, the lack of relevant precedents and the fact that conventional approaches offer few or no policy suggestions for solving the hard cases at hand. But

© The Author(s) 2017
P. Mindus, *European Citizenship after Brexit*, Palgrave Studies in European Union Politics, DOI 10.1007/978-3-319-51774-2_4

45

there are also more deep-seated reasons why a different kind of approach to the matter is needed. Some are starting to sense that a choice has to be made: Are we serious about the exit or about safeguarding rights? In what follows, four arguments are made in favour of a theoretical take.

The first reason is dictated by circumstance: the political volatility surrounding the matter suggests avoiding predictive activities. It is imperative to determine if, and which, 'acquired rights' will be upheld – in itself a 'dauting task,' to use the phrasing adopted by the EU committee report, entitled *The Process of Withdrawing from the European Union* and drafted at the request of the House of Lords in 2015 (House of Lords 2015).

As things currently stand, outcomes of negotiations cannot be foreseen. Focus here will be on determining what resources, if any, are available to the legal scholar regardless of what may happen politically. I will therefore operate under the assumption agreement-less withdrawal.

Many have pointed out the unlikelihood of non-negotiated withdrawal. Yet, in this study I will discuss this possibility (or a withdrawal treaty making no mention of free movement rights, which for the present purposes would amount to the same thing). I have chosen to operate under this assumption because the question of remedies in the absence of an agreement is relevant since there is no guarantee that any agreement would have terms that are favourable to all affected groups and/or that any agreement would claim comprehensiveness.

In the next chapter of the book, I scrutinise the extra-negotiational resources able to 'freeze' what is often described as the 'transnational individual rights of EU citizens' so as to point out some limits to political engineering. Despite the unquestionable existence and importance of the political dimension, the primary focus is on the legal nature of the consequences of Brexit for the laws governing nationality, EU citizenship status and connected rights.

The second reason that suggests we avoid adopting mechanically the approaches we find in mainstream legal research is the *unprecedented character* of Brexit. The very framing of the unprecedented nature of the problem requires some reflection and it raises a number of very important issues, a point which was made clear in the wake of the High Court's decision on 3 November 2016 concerning the issue of whether the government needs to obtain approval from Parliament to trigger Article 50 (see, e.g. Peers 2016). There is much novelty in what is happening: Invoking Article 50 is certainly uncharted territory (Craig 2016).

It is not, however, the first time in the history of European integration that the territorial scope of application of the Treatises changes. Previous modification of territorial validity include the following: In 1975 the EC Treaties ceased to cover the French Commodores and the island of Mayotte, which however is now EU overseas territory; the same happened in Dutch New Guinea (1962); Algeria (1962); Greenland (1985); Saint Barthémely (2003). European integration history also includes cases of member state territory declared to fall outside the scope of the Treatises: suffice to mention, for example, Faroe, Macao, Hong Kong, Surinam and the UK Sovereign Base Areas in Cyprus, as well as territories that joined after the member state joined: for example, Netherlands Antilles and the Canary Islands (Kochenov 2011). To be precise, more than half of what used to be member states' territory have 'left' since the creation of the Communities (Ziller 2005). The reference is to the Belgian territories of Congo, Rwanda-Burundi, Italian protectorate of Somalia, the Netherlands, New Guinea, French equatorial Africa, French East-Africa, the protectorates of Togo and Cameroon, the Commodores Islands, Madagascar, the Côte Française des Somalis; and following the accession of the UK, also Bahamas, Brunei, the Caribbean Colonies and Associated States, Gilbert and Ellis islands, the Line Islands, the Anglo-French condominium of the New Hebrides, the Solomon Islands and the Seychelles.

Yet, there is no *relevant* precedent, when reviewing the territorial changes that have taken place in the 'territory of the Union,' which can be applied in strict analogy to Brexit. Not even the independence of Algeria, the 'withdrawal' of Greenland, nor the most recent modification of EU territory, that is, the case of Saint Barthélemy, can be fully compared with Brexit. Saint Barthémely had a previous status as *départment* belonging to Guadaloupe, but after the 2003 referendum the island became a 'communauté d'outre mer' as defined in Art. 79 *Constitution Française*.

Algeria would probably be the closest precedent, if any were to be indicated. Yet, the events were such that the analogy does not hold: Between 1962 and 1975, when Algeria concluded a treaty with the EEC, the Treaties were nonetheless 'valid by implication' (sic!), but Algerians lost the status of member state nationals for the purposes of Community law (Laffont 1979). In February 2004 the European Commission answered a parliamentary question that queried the precedential value of Algerian independence for a division of a member state and whether the region in question would have to leave the EU and renegotiate an accession treaty and the answer was that a part of member state territory upon gaining independence is from EU perspective a third country in which EU law is not valid. *A fortiori*, this is the case of a receding state.

Greenland is often mentioned in the media and by certain scholars, but it is even more misleading. Greenland never did exit. Following a vote in 1982, Greenland officially 'withdrew' from the European communities in 1985. There were difficult and protracted negotiations between the governments of Greenland and Denmark, and between Denmark and the Commission, particularly with regard to fisheries. Greenland became associated with the EU as an Overseas Country and Territory (OCT) through the Greenland Treaty.[1] The Article 2 of the Protocol attached to the Greenland Treaty clarified that there would be a transitional period during which Greenlanders, non-national residents and businesses with acquired rights under EU law would retain these rights.[2] The agreement applied to Greenland is hard to define as any kind of 'exit.' Greenland simply changed its status under the Treaties to an Overseas Country or Territory in the sense of Annex II.

Another reason why the analogy with Greenland fails is political: Because the Brexit debate regarded immigration, we should rule out that, were the UK to leave without any negotiated transitional measures, it would retain free movement *tout court*. When Greenland 'left' the EU, the Commission considered that vested rights meant Greenland should retain 'the substance' of free movement rights for workers from other EC countries employed in Greenland at the time of withdrawal:

Provision should be made for appropriate measures to protect companies and persons who have exercised the right of establishment as well as Community workers employed in Greenland. The extremely small number of persons affected and the case-law of the Court of Justice that has already been established in favour of the retention of pension rights acquired by workers during periods of employment in a territory which has subsequently ceased to belong to the Community give no reason to suppose that there will be any major difficulties in this area, even if the future status of Greenland were to rule out the principle of free movement. It would, however, be preferable to retain the substance of the Community rules, at least in respect of Community workers employed in Greenland at the time of withdrawal.[3]

The Commission did not say whether the rest of the EU should retain these rights for workers from Greenland.

None of the cases mentioned can be said to constitute precedents. This fact suggests that traditional comparative legal readings may therefore be inappropriate.

Let alone the political volatility and the unprecedented character of the case at hand, there is a third reason suggesting we adopt a better-reasoned approach. It pertains to the legal uncertainty affecting many on both sides of the emerging border. The complexities involved in finding remedial solutions calls for an assessment that avoids jumping to incautious conclusions. A complete overview of remedial options to enforce 'vested rights' in EU27 for UK nationals stripped of Treaty rights is a complicated affair. It is a matter of national law that would depend on the individual provisions of each member state's domestic public and administrative law.

The conventional wisdom has it that Union citizenship follows national citizenship like a shadow follows the body that carries it along. From here springs the commonly made assumption that entitlements vanish when access criteria are no longer fulfilled. This is, in my view, due to the way citizenship is, often but not always, conceived in legal science. Most lawyers confuse the meaning of *status civitatis* with criteria for access and loss of the status.[4] Indeed, ask 'what is citizenship?' and the standard answer will invariably involve reference to the principles of *ius soli* and *ius sanguinis* that regulate access criteria. This instinctive reaction leads to the often-repeated claim that no treaty rights can thus be guaranteed to those who are *ipso facto* no longer European citizens: Good riddance to the Treaty rights of Brits living in the Union! Neither can Treaty rights be enforced beyond the scope of application of the Treatises: Good luck to European citizens in the UK! This approach undermines the search for smart policy suggestions. I prefer to offer a better-informed view of the relationship between loss of the status, and the content of European citizenship. *Status civitatis*, after all, is a conceptual bridge linking the criteria for acquisition and loss to the entitlements the status consists in.

Finally, a last reason to think well about the way we approach the issue of Brexit depends on the fact that the stakes are high. This is not only due to the foreshadowed political circumstances, general novelty and legal ambiguity but also due to the very significance of Brexit for Union citizenship. The way issues raised by Brexit, especially in relation to 'citizenship rights,' will be tackled is revealing of the nature of Union citizenship and of the strength, or weakness, of the vertical link between the Union and *its* citizens. Who has the competence to withdraw the status of Union citizenship? What are the limits to the 'sovereign right to exclude'? Are these limits sufficient for making the case that European citizenship is 'the fundamental status' of 'those who find themselves in the same situation to enjoy the same treatment in law irrespective of their nationality'[5] according to a federal-constitutional reading?[6] Or do these limits show that the 'rights' attached to the status are more truthfully framed, in the intergovernmental perspective on European citizenship, as 'privileges' or 'concessions' that are 'mutually recognised'?[7] Looking into the extra-negotiational resources for 'freezing rights' is important from this perspective because to answer these questions means to confront a dilemma:

One horn of the dilemma is constituted by the claim that supranational rights constitute European citizenship and cannot be erased at will by the withdrawing state; the other horn is constituted by the claim that they may very well be suppressed if a member state decides to exit. The European Court of Justice (ECJ) stated back in 1963 in the case *Van Gend and Loos* that such rights are part of individuals' 'legal heritage.' Would this imply that 'such acquired rights cannot be immediately and directly extinguished'? (Douglas-Scott 2015). Will rights exercised under EU law be recognised as part of individuals' legal heritage, outlasting the legal provisions that created it? Or would such a reading violate the very spirit of exiting, according to the view that 'imposing [European citizenship and relative rights-protection] on the people of a member state who just voted to leave the Union would be nothing but a direct attack on the letter and purpose of the provision making withdrawals possible'? (Kochenov 2016; also Athanassiou and Laulhé Shaelou 2016). Can't the 'acquired rights' of people having made use of their free movement be frozen without rending futile the attempt of a country to exit the Union? Would such a freezing mean that European citizenship deprives Article 50 of its *effet utile*? To some, the issue is nothing less than a constitutional test: 'The de-coupling of European from national citizenship in the CJEU's case-law has already begun to shift citizens' entitlement to jointly decide about membership in the polity from the national to the European level. Extending that primordial political right to the case of the UK leaving the Union would certainly amount to a *coup d'état*' (Dawson and Augenstein 2016).

Put this way, the dilemma looks like a choice between Scylla and Charybdis: Sacrificing EU citizens' rights on the altar of democratic self-determination or – if rights are substantially maintained and content of

Union citizenship left unaltered – sacrifice the will of the people to withdraw on the altar of individual rights. The risk of facing such a dilemma warrants the rest of this inquiry.

4.2 APPLYING CITIZENSHIP THEORY TO BREXIT

4.2.1 The Functionalist Theory

Citizenship, conceptually speaking, is a so-called middle-term.[8] This is the starting point of the functionalist theory of citizenship, which is a general theory of citizenship that provides a framework for *de lege ferenda* analysis of citizenship laws. A general theory of citizenship, to be such, needs to describe the relationship between entitlements and access criteria. Entitlements are about *what* citizenship consists in. Access criteria determine to *whom* the status is conferred. These two dimensions constitute the concept's extension and intension, in the philosophical sense.

Extension is determined by answering the query 'Who is the citizen?' To answer such a query is to give a list of criteria for acquisition and loss of the status. These criteria give us information about which persons are *denoted* by the term. *Intension* is determined by the query 'What is a citizen?' To answer such a query is to indicate a set of entitlements or legal positions – typically rights and duties. To determine *intension* is therefore to indicate the *content* of citizenship. *Intension*, in other words, defines the properties *connoted* by citizenship.

Both intension and extension vary. This has led many to conclude that we cannot know beforehand anything about the variation. This is wrong. The two dimensions do not vary indefinitely. Their variation is intelligible and can be studied. The illusion of indefinite and rationally uncontrollable variation arises when one studies one dimension of citizenship separately from the other.

Emboldened by this insight, the functionalist theory develops two ideas: The constitutional-sensitivity thesis and the correlation thesis.

The constitutional-sensitivity thesis submits that information on citizenship, in its combined form, consisting both of access criteria and entitlements, is a source of *constitutional meta-data*: The variation of extension (i.e. criteria for acquisition and loss) in relation to intension (i.e. legal positions associated with the status) provides information about the constitutional identity of a polity. This is so because nationality law is not just any area of law. The power to define the *demos*, to determine who counts as citizens – the flip side of the state's 'power to exclude'[9] – is essential to the existence and identity of the state. There is a correlation between the role of the citizenry and nature of the polity (Mindus 2016). To define this role attention needs to be paid to both entitlements connected to the status and criteria for acquisition and loss. Access to citizenship regulates how the *demos* (or set of citizens) is composed; and entitlements determine their share of power. The composition and role of the *demos* in a legal order is determinative of its constitutional identity. Ever since Aristotle, the number of people allowed to hold office and share political power constitutes a measure defining the form of government.[10] This is the fundamental intuition behind the constitutional-sensitivity thesis.

According to the correlation thesis, access to *status civitatis* is not neutral, but can be conceived as a variable of the content of the status. There is a relationship between the two dimensions that is best described as a *functional correlation*, in the mathematical meaning of function. This correlation is functional in the sense that criteria giving access to the status and the type of entitlements it entails have to be aligned so that access criteria fit the particular type of entitlements connected to the status. If they are not aligned by functional correlation, citizenship becomes an arbitrary instrument of social closure: As if we were to distinguish insiders from outsiders randomly. Who is eligible for citizenship is a question that depends on the features required to enjoy the entitlements and perform the duties of citizenship. Which characteristics, capabilities, distinctive features are relevant, and reasonable to require, depends on the type of rights and obligations that a given 'citizenship' consists in. Therefore access to the status is functionally correlated to the content of it. Changing one impacts the other. The functional correlation can be expressed as follows:

I use the term *codomain* (C) to refer to extension (i.e. criteria for acquisition and loss of citizenship) and *domain* (D) to refer to intension (entitlements or legal positions associated with the status). Both are non-empty sets.[11] The domain is the set of the arguments for which the function is defined; the codomain is the target set. No submission is made about cardinality at this stage.

$$C = \{c_1, c_2 ... c_n\}$$
$$D = \{d_1, d_2, ... d_n\}$$

The *correlation thesis* claims that criteria for acquisition and loss of the status constitute a function of the entitlements it consists in. Symbolically, it can be summarised in the following way:

$$f : D \twoheadrightarrow C$$

In other words, f is a surjective function from D to C so that:

$$\forall c \in C, \exists d \in D, f(d) = c$$

The function is surjective because every point in the codomain is the value of $f(d)$ for at least one point d in the domain.

We can operate in two ways to better understand a particular case of *status civitatis*. Given a set of criteria of acquisition and loss, the intension that can be connected to such an extension may be inferred. Otherwise said, if we have knowledge about criteria for acquisition and loss, we may infer compatible entitlements. Given a set of entitlements, we may deduce what extension fits this intension. In other words, if we know what a given citizenship consists in (i.e. the rights and duties that are connected to the status) we are in a position to tell, consistently with the content of the status, which criteria for acquisition and loss are consistent with the entitlements.

If the characterisation of the relationship between *intension* (D) and *extension* (C) in terms of functional correlation is correct, we obtain a *standard* for evaluating the appropriateness of criteria for acquisition and loss. We can thus analyse the internal consistency of the design of a given citizenship policy. The functionalist theory offers a standard against which we can test whether granting citizenship is justified; or, if you prefer, a standard allowing for principled reasoning about the design of citizenship laws.

If the design is to be consistent, extension will follow intension in such a way that to *who* citizenship is granted must depend on *what* citizenship consists in. Here are three examples taken from well-known approaches to citizenship. First example: If we assume that the intension is given by, for example, political autonomy, it is consistent that extension is determined by, for example, adulthood (proxy for maturity). Therefore, age is a reasonable criterion for access to franchise. Second example: If the intension is given by, for example, subjecthood to the legal order, then it is consistent that extension is determined by, for example, birth on the territory (proxy for physical presence). Therefore, *ius soli* is a reasonable for criterion for acquisition of citizenship. Third example: If the intension is given by, for example, ensuring transgenerational solidarity, then it is consistent that extension is determined by, for example, descent or family ties. Therefore, *ius sanguinis* is a reasonable criterion for acquisition of citizenship.

It is important to notice that the standard is not reliant on factors that vary with the observer, for example, political opinion, worldview, conceptions of the good and more. It relies on internal consistency between input data (i.e. which legal positions – rights and duties – a given citizenship consists of) and output data (i.e. criteria for acquisition and loss).

4.2.2   How Can it be Applied to Brexit?

From the functional perspective, EU citizenship is more similar to national citizenships than one might expect, notwithstanding the wording of the annexed Declaration to the Danish Act of Ratification of the Maastricht Treaty that states: 'Nothing in the Treaty on European Union implies or foresees an undertaking to create a citizenship of the Union in the sense of a citizenship of a nation-state.'[12] Conceptually, both are middle-terms allowing connection between, on the one hand, criteria determining acquisition and loss and, on the other, entitlements associated with the status.

In keeping with the theory, we should start by distinguishing between, on the one hand, criteria determining access to the status and, on the other, the content of citizenship. It enables to visualise the characteristic bi-dimensionality of citizenship. We can thus see how the problem of vested or acquired rights emerges in the first place: The EU citizenship status, created by the EU Treaties, may be additional and thus have no independent existence following a State's withdrawal from the EU for the nationals of that member state, but the material implication need not be that rights of citizens disappear.

The bi-dimensionality of citizenship shows gaps and asymmetries that arise between having access to the status and enjoying the rights connected to it. Such asymmetries are normatively suspicious (they lower the internal consistency of the status) but they sometimes appear as a matter of legal fact. The bi-dimensionality of citizenship explains why the consequences of constitutional territorial permutations for the enjoyment of supranational rights are not straightforward. Possession of citizenship status is non-territorial, even though rights attached to the status may be territorial.

Bi-dimensionality may thus demonstrate how state succession produces new foreigners who are affected by 'quasi-loss' of EU citizenship status (or invalidation *ex tunc* of the status) resulting in the impossibility to access rights.[13] Bi-dimensionality also explains the asymmetries involved in cases in which people lost rights without losing the status due to racist immigration policies;[14] or how others have the status but with a reduction of its content, like Manxmen and Channel Islanders who may vote for the European Parliament but are prohibited from free movement unless they reside five years in the UK; or how the Faroe islanders never had the status but *de facto* access (some) rights. The people of the Faroe Islands are Danes but not EU citizens. The Danish government added a protocol specifying that 'the Danish nationals' of the islands were not 'nationals for the purposes of Community law'[15] – which is basically the predecessor status of Union citizenship. Yet this limitation of the scope of application has virtually no impact on the Faroe islanders: 'Given that limitation was merely territorial, there is no evidence that it has in any way affected the enjoyment of EU citizenship by the Faroe islanders, as long as they do not travel on the green Faroe model of the Danish passport, which they can, but are not obliged to request' (Kochenov 2016).

Such asymmetries are easily spotted on the background of the bi-dimensionality that the functionalist theory builds on.

From a normative standpoint, the functionalist theory also holds such gaps to be unwarranted. The core design idea of the functionalist theory, as foreshowed above, is that legitimacy is dictated by fittingness of criteria (for acquisition and loss) to content. Depending on which entitlements are considered to be determinative of the content of EU citizenship, the relevant feature that people need to have to access these rights will change. This reflects on criteria for loss of the status as well. Such criteria stand in functional correlation to the content of citizenship in the same way as criteria determining acquisition. A first indication of this is of course that the rules on loss of citizenship vary remarkably across states, at least as much as the rules on the acquisition of citizenship (Vink and De Groot 2010; Vink and Chun Luk 2015). Consider, for example, the following:

Insofar as the entitlement that European citizenship is connected with is, say, the special right to consular protection, then a relevant feature is reciprocity of recognition or equal privileges, for which – commonly and not unreasonably – having the nationality of a member state is taken to be a proxy. Reasoning under such an assumption means it would be legitimate to withdraw European citizenship because there is no reciprocity of recognition on grounds of nationality (since, in the event of Brexit, the UK would no longer be a member state). It is so precisely because the entitlement attached to the status basically is a privilege to which one may cling only insofar as the reciprocity ground is upheld.

Insofar as the entitlements connected to European citizenship are such that the status is *destined to be the fundamental status of Member State nationals* – to use a famous phrasing of the ECJ – then, a relevant feature would be that of being fundamentally linked to, or affected by, the Union. Affectedness may stand as a proxy for 'having ties to.' Entitlements would not amount to mere privileges or special rights, but would need to embody supranational features. A case in point is supranational political rights. It would be legitimate to withdraw the status from those who no longer are affected by EU law but it would be illegitimate to withdraw the status from those who are enjoying it as long as they are affected. Will post-Europeans be affected by EU law? If they live in the Union, they surely will. Consequently, to strip them of their 'fundamental status' would be illegitimate. If they do not live in the Union the situation is different. It might be illegitimate to withdraw the status of those whose rights are frozen, depending on which these are. It will turn, in part, on which rights are frozen and whether the loss of status can be challenged.

Depending on what is held to be the content of European citizenship, criteria for withdrawal of the status will vary. The functionalist theory provides us with a standard against which we can test under which conditions withdrawal is legitimate.

But it also provides information in the other direction: Given a set of criteria for acquisition and loss, we may infer knowledge of the nature and type of entitlements compatible with such a set.[16] The same is true for criteria determining loss. Under which conditions is withdrawal of status (il)legitimate? Answering provides an indirect source of information about which entitlements are attached to the status.

Both of these directions are important when we want to understand European citizenship after Brexit: *If loss can be determined solely at domestic level, are entitlements still supranational rights? Vice versa, if entitlements are supranational individual rights, can loss be univocally determined by a Member State?* In the next two chapters I explore both directions of inquiry. In the final chapter, I draw some conclusions about the nature of Union citizenship.

Consistently with the theory, 'who gets to judge legitimacy of withdrawal of supranational entitlements?' is a question the answer to which cannot be any member state that so wishes. *A fortiori*, this authority cannot lie with a former member state – who would then have full authority to judge over the legitimacy of withdrawal of supranational entitlements in a Union of which it is no longer part! If loss is imposed unilaterally and unconditionally by a member state, it is an indication of the fact that the entitlements that the status consists in are at most mutually recognised privileges. If grounds for loss are not unilaterally determined at domestic level, this very fact can be taken as an indication of, albeit not full proof of, the supranational nature of at least some entitlements.

Without looking to pre-empt the results of my inquiry in the next sections, it turns out that as far as *criteria* determining loss are concerned, there are limits to what States can do, even within their *domaine réservé* and this may prove to have repercussions in domestic legislation even after exit. In particular, the UK has strong incentive to reform its nationality and immigration law to avoid instrumental naturalisation and abuse of multiple citizenships. But European law imposes limits to what the UK can do to protect itself against this indirect way of undermining the point of Brexit. There are also things that the (citizenry of the) Union could do. As far as *content* is concerned, (some) rights may be frozen, but they are not those making Union citizenship a supranational legal status. The legal grounds enabling freezing are international, not European. This will be so at least until the EU adheres to the European Convention of Human Rights, an idea that lost traction in the wake of the ECJ's *Opinion 2/13* from 2014. Other rights can be saved, but it would require decoupling the concepts of nationality and Union citizenship. If the EU sees Union citizenship as a fundamental status, it need not depend on the idiosyncrasies of the application of domestic nationality laws. In Brexit, to save the supranational rights connected to Union citizenship, certain groups of people who lose member state nationality would need to keep their connection to the Union. The windows of legal opportunity for such creative solutions are very small. To determine which, let us see how rights can be frozen.

NOTES

1. OJ L 29, 1 February 1985.
2. See also *Status of Greenland: Commission opinion*, COM (83) 66 final, 2 February 1983.

3. Quote from House of Commons 2013, at 15.
4. See Mindus 2014, third chapter on definitions in legal science.
5. Case C-184/99 *Rudy Grzelczyk v. Centre public d'aide sociale d'Ottignies-Louvain-la-neuve* (2001) ECR I-6193, § 31. But also Case C-224/98 *D'Hoop* [2002] ECR I-6191 § 28; Case C-148/02 *Avello* [2003] ECR I-1161 § 22; Case C-403/03 *Schempp* [2005] ECR I-6421 § 15.
6. On the evolution of the two major frameworks for assessing European integration, see de Búrca 2012, esp. at 126 ff.
7. The literature on mutual recognition is growing: see Lenaerts 2015; Janssens 2013; Möstl 2010; Schmidt 2008; Nicolaïdis 2007; Padoa Schioppa 2005.
8. Middle-terms are neither true nor false. They are to be retained if they make a consistent connection between premises and conclusions. They are to be rejected otherwise.
9. The formula was coined by the US Supreme Court in *Trop v. Dulles*, 356 U.S. 86, 101 (1958), at 355.
10. Aristotle combines quantitative and qualitative criteria in his theory on forms of government. The two criteria are: number of citizens sharing political power and whether power is exercised in the interest of the power-holder. See Mindus 2014, Chapter 2.
11. In what follows I shall express the relation between *intension* (Domain) and *extension* (Codomain) in mathematical terms borrowed from naïve set theory: see Halmos 1960.
12. Declaration on the citizenship of the Union to be associated to the Danish Act of Ratification [1992] OJ C348/1.
13. For example, *Kaur* (16 Case C-192/99 The Queen v Secretary of State for the Home Department, ex parte: Manjit Kaur [2001] ECR I-01237), a case involving a third country national who was recognised by the UK as citizen of the UK and Colonies but did not fall within the personal scope of rules relating to citizens entitled to reside in the UK, she could not rely on her Union citizenship. The European Court of Justice held that Kaur never had been a European citizen so rights never arose in the first place.
14. For example, the case of East Africans Asians in the UK. See Lester 2003.
15. *Protocol n. 2 to the Act of Accession, relating to the Faro Islands, art. 4, 1972* (OJ L 73 163).
16. There is a degree of imprecision in this since citizenship constitutes a surjective function: every ground for loss (or point in the codomain) is the value of $f(d)$ for at least one point d in the domain (or entitlement connected to the status). But adjustments are done at a later stage: in reflexive equilibrium between what we know about the contents of citizenship respective of what we know about the criteria for acquisition and loss.

REFERENCES

Athanassiou, P., Laulhé Shaelou, S. (2016) 'EU Citizenship and its Relevance for EU Exit and Secession', in D. Kochenov (ed.) *EU Citizenship and Federalism: The Role of Rights*, Cambridge: CUP (forthcoming).

Craig, P. (2016) Brexit: A Drama in Six Acts (11 July 2016) *European Law Review* August 2016, available at: http://papers.ssrn.com/sol3/papers.cfm?abstract_id=2807975 (last accessed 30 October 2016).

Dawson, M., Augenstein, D., 'After Brexit: Time for a Further Decoupling of European and National Citizenship?', *VerfBlog*, 14 July 2016, available at http://verfassungsblog.de/brexit-decoupling-european-national-citizenship/ (last accessed 30 October 2016).

De Búrca, G. (2012) 'The ECJ and the International Legal Order: A Re-evaluation', in G. De Búrca, J.H.H. Weiler (eds.) *The Worlds of European Constitutionalism*, Cambridge: CUP.

Douglas-Scott, S. (2015) 'Constitutional Implications of a UK Exit from the EU: Some Questions that Really Must be Asked', U.K. Const. L. Blog, (17 April 2015), available at https://ukconstitutionallaw.org/2015/04/17/sionaidh-douglas-scott-constitutional-implications-of-a-uk-exit-from-the-eu-some-questions-that-really-must-be-asked/ (last accessed 30 October 2016).

Halmos, P. (1960) *Naive Set Theory*, Dordrecht: Springer.

House of Commons (2013) *Leaving the EU Report of House of Commons*, available at http://researchbriefings.parliament.uk/ResearchBriefing/Summary/RP13-42#fullreport (last accessed 30 October 2016).

House of Lords EU Committee Report on *The Process of Withdrawing from the European Union* 11th Report of Session 2015–16, available at: http://www.publications.parliament.uk/pa/ld201516/ldselect/ldeucom/138/138.pdf (last accessed 30 October 2016).

Janssens, C. (2013) *The Principle of Mutual Recognition in EU Law*, Oxford: Oxford University Press.

Kochenov, D. (2011) *EU Law of the Overseas*, Dordrecht: Kluwer Law International.

Kochenov, D. (2016) *EU Citizenship and Withdrawals from the Union: How Inevitable is the Radical Downgrading of Rights?*, LEQS Paper No. 111/2016, available at http://www.lse.ac.uk/europeanInstitute/LEQS%20Discussion%20Paper%20Series/LEQSPaper111.pdf (last accessed 30 October 2016).

Laffont, P. (1979) *Histoire de la France en Algérie*, Paris: Plon.

Lenaerts, K. (2015) 'The Principle of Mutual Recognition in the Area of Freedom, Security and Justice', The Fourth Annual Sir Jeremy Lever Lecture, University of Oxford, 30 January 2015, available at https://www.law.ox.ac.uk/sites/files/oxlaw/the_principle_of_mutual_recognition_in_the_area_of_freedom_judge_lenaerts.pdf (last accessed 30 October 2016).

Lester, A. (2003) Lord of Herne Hill QC, Lecture, *East Africans Asians vs UK: The Inside Story*, 23 October 2003.

Mindus, P. (2014) *Cittadini e no. Forme e funzioni dell'inclusione e dell'esclusione*, Florence: Firenze University Press.

Mindus, P. (2016) 'Citizenship and Arbitrary Law-Making: On the Quaintness of Non-national Disenfranchisement', 7 *Società Mutamento Politica* 13, Special Issue 'Citizenships of Our Times', available at http://www.fupress.net/index. php/smp/article/view/18287/16968 (last accessed 30 October 2016).

Möstl, M. (2010) 'Preconditions and Limits of Mutual Recognition', 47 *Common Market Law Review* 405–436.

Nicolaïdis, K. (2007) 'Kir Forever? The Journey of a Political Scientist in the Landscape of Recognition', in M.P. Maduro (ed.) *The Past and Future of EU Law. The Classics of EU Law Revisited on the 50th Anniversary of the Rome Treaty*, Hart: Oxford.

Padoa Schioppa, F.K. (ed.) (2005) *The Principle of Mutual Recognition in the European Integration Process*, Basingstoke: Palgrave McMillan.

Peers, S. (2016) 'Brexit: Can the ECJ Get Involved?', Blog entry at EU law analysis from 3 November 2016, available at http://eulawanalysis.blogspot.it/2016/ 11/brexit-can-ecj-get-involved.html (last accessed 7 November 2016).

Schmidt, S. (ed.) (2008) *Mutual Recognition as a New Mode of Governance*, London: Routledge.

Vink, M.P., Chun Luk, N. (2015) 'Mapping Statistics on Loss of Nationality in the EU: A New Online Database', in S. Carrera Nunez, G.-R. De Groot (eds.) *European Citizenship at the Crossroads*, Oisterwijk: Wolf.

Vink, M.P., De Groot, G.R. (2010) *Birthright-Based Acquisition of Citizenship*, EUDO Citizenship Comparative Analysis, RSCAS/EUDO-CIT-Comp. 2010/6, available at http://eudo-citizenship.eu/docs/Vink_DeGroot.pdf (last accessed 30 October 2016).

Ziller, J. (2005) 'L'Union Européenne et l'outre-mer', 113 *Pouvoirs* 145.

CHAPTER 5

Can Rights Be Frozen?

Abstract This chapter focuses on the intension of Union citizenship by asking if rights can be frozen. In particular, we look at the extra-negotiational legal resources available for freezing rights of the people involved. Can rights be frozen? Which rights? Whose rights? Under what conditions? For how long? Sources of international law and EU law, including guidelines from lesser-known sources and doctrinal instruments, are taken into account. The conclusion is that some rights of some of the people involved will be frozen, but that the legal grounds for doing so suggests that Union citizenship is not what the European Court of Justice and most scholars claim it is.

Keywords European citizenship · Functionalist theory of citizenship · Brexit · Freedom of movement · Right of residence · EU law · Migration law · International law

This chapter explores the content side of citizenship, its intension. Let us turn to entitlements and ask if rights can be frozen. In particular, we look at the extra-negotiational legal resources available for freezing rights of the people involved. Can rights be frozen? Which rights? Whose rights? Under what conditions? For how long? On what grounds?

We examine sources of international law and EU law, including guidelines from lesser-known sources and doctrinal instruments. To do so, analogous reasoning will be applied to the unprecedented situation.[1]

© The Author(s) 2017   61
P. Mindus, *European Citizenship after Brexit*, Palgrave Studies
in European Union Politics, DOI 10.1007/978-3-319-51774-2_5

Analogy is never a purely logical argument and ought to be taken *cum granu salis.*[2] More modestly, analogies explored here will merely help to enucleate guidelines.

The conclusion is that some rights of some of the people involved can be frozen, but that the legal grounds for doing so suggests that Union citizenship is not what the European Court of Justice and most scholars claim it is.

5.1   LESSONS FROM INTERNATIONAL LAW

International law does not regulate explicitly a matter like the loss of European citizenship for UK citizens, nor the loss of territorial EU citizenship rights for second country nationals in the UK. Some have argued that British expats in the Union would have 'acquired rights' under the 1969 Vienna Convention on the Law of Treaties (VCLT). Reference is to vested rights under Article 70(1)(b) VCLT and to the formula '(b) does not affect any right, obligation or legal situation of the parties created through the execution of the treaty prior to its termination.' This source of international law is an unlikely candidate for protecting acquired rights.[3] It is unclear, to say the least, if such a notion could be used in the first place; if it would cover the situation; if it would cover all rights; or else, which rights? whose rights? and with what exact practical impact? Retaining 'executed' rights – that is, those rights that are not automatically revoked if a treaty or law no longer applies, and that can be retained even in the event of a change in the ultimate power over a country – refers to 'private' rights, whereas EU citizens' rights include highly 'public' rights, for example, voting and standing in elections at local and European level. Not much solace is to be found in this reference to international law.

The ban on arbitrary deprivation of citizenship recurrent in many international instruments – others venture – might have some bearing: As things currently stand, 'questions are bound to arise, should the withdrawing state be willing to retroactively terminate the rights enjoyed by EU citizens connected with other member states in its own territory' (Kochenov 2016). Yet, it would be limited to cases of retroactive restrictions and would therefore be silent on the situation of post-exit restrictions.

Can international law at least provide us with guidelines as to what happens to Union citizenship in the case at hand? If we look at how nationality matters have been regulated in state succession scenarios, some interpretative aids may be distilled. The analogical reasoning is warranted by the fact that the problems, which secessions pose to citizenship at the national level, are very similar to the problems posed by withdrawals from the EU in relation to Union citizenship (Closa 2014), even though there are limits to the analogy: The EU is not a state; it is difficult to argue for the existence of a change in sovereignty; no new nationality law needs to be written. Previous experiences cannot easily be made to fit Brexit, especially considering the emphasis of the European Court of Justice on Union citizenship being the fundamental status of nationals of member states.

There are three lessons to learn from the state succession literature as far as guiding principles are concerned: The leaving country and the remaining bloc have a duty to negotiate solutions, the leaving country has a duty to inform and possibly to suggest options for individuals concerned.

5.1.1 Duty to Negotiate Solutions

From the legal doctrine on succession, we learn that there is a general obligation to seek negotiated solutions. Consider, for example, Article 19 of the *European Convention on Nationality* from 1997 (ECN) that substantially repeats the Art. 10(1) of the 1961 *Convention on Statelessness.* 'In cases of state succession, state parties concerned shall endeavour to regulate matters relating to nationality by agreement amongst themselves and, where applicable, in their relationship with other States concerned.' The 'duty' of reaching negotiated solutions is a consistent feature of international instruments dealing with state succession. In September 2012 the Union made a formal pledge that all member states will consider ratification.[4] The UK, however, has not signed: 'The 'duty' to negotiate is also reinforced at EU level on the side of the predecessor EU member state which must observe the principle of proportionality [and other general principles of EU law] when drafting the new nationality legislation in the event of the independence of part of its territory' (Gonzalez Marrero 2016, 108).

The obligation to negotiate was also mentioned in the decision of the Supreme Court of Canada *Reference re Secession of Quebec.* In the advisory Opinion by the Canadian Supreme Court issued at request of the government on the issue of secession of Quebec, the court found that:

> the federalist principle, in conjunction with the democratic principle, dictates that the clear repudiation of the existing constitutional order and the clear

expression of the desire to pursue secession by the population of a province would give rise to a reciprocal obligation on all parties to the Confederation to negotiate constitutional changes to respond to that desire (...). The corollary (...) is an obligation on all parties to come to the negotiation table.[5]

There may thus be a constraint on the possibilities of limiting 'acquired rights' of UK nationals in EU27. It has been suggested that 'UK citizens in the EU would have a legal position inferior to Russians and Moroccans (whose countries have non-discrimination agreements with the EU)' (Kochenov 2016) but the duty to negotiate solutions would not be compatible with such treatment.

5.1.2   Duty to Inform

An interesting source relating to this guideline is the UN International Law Commission's *Draft Articles on Nationality of Natural Persons in Relation to the Succession of States* from 1999.[6] The Draft Articles require all appropriate steps to be taken to 'ensure persons concerned will be informed, within a reasonable time period, of the effect of its legislation on their nationality' (Art. 6). It is not unreasonable to assume that it would be valid also in the event of exit from international organisation such as the EU. The rationale of the duty to inform is that persons concerned 'should not be reduced to a purely passive role as regards the impact of the succession of States on their individual status or confronted with adverse effects of the exercise of a right of option of which they could objectively have no knowledge when exercising such a right.'[7] The Draft Articles are not binding and, after deferral, the topic has disappeared from the UN general assembly's agenda. This source may nonetheless be said to provide relevant guidelines.

In event of Brexit, the UK would need to inform persons concerned, that is, both second country nationals in the UK and British nationals in the Union of 'the effect of its legislation on their nationality.' This duty to inform does not seem to have been considered. It can be read as a limit to using citizens of either side as 'bargaining chips in negotiations' contrarily to suggestions made by several British politicians, including Theresa May, at the end of June and repeated on several occasions. This position was not modified in the speech on the Brexit plan delivered at Lancaster House 17 January 2017. Indeed, merely leaving it up for behind closed-door negotiations to settle the issue would potentially deprived 'persons concerned' of knowledge of 'the effect of [the] legislation on their nationality.' Exchange of information and consultations between States are fundamental to identify the negative consequences that may arise for the status of the persons concerned and for the issues linked to the status. There is an 'obligation' – of positive morality, to use Austin's phrase – to provide clearness on nationality matters (promotion of legal certainty) so as to reduce the number of potential hard cases and secure, as far as possible, rights acquired under the previous legal setting.

5.1.3 Right to Option

States involved in succession shall give consideration to the will of persons concerned especially nationals of the predecessor state. Article 18 of the *European Convention on Nationality* formulates a list of criteria to be taken into account in case of state succession, without indicating a principle for weighting these. One criterion to be reckoned with is 'the will of the person.' This source binds 13 member states, but not the UK. This guideline, however, also appears in other sources: Art. 24 and 25 of the Involuntary Loss of European Citizenship *Draft Articles* also provide for the predecessor state to deprive persons of 'old' citizenship in case they acquire the successor state's nationality – 'unless otherwise indicated by the exercise of *a right of option*.' The possible consequences that may derive from the non-binding guideline centred on providing a right to option is less clear than the previous two guidelines. What would a right to option be in the Brexit case? In case of state succession within the EU, for example, Scotland, Flanders or Catalonia, the choice would be between Scottish and British, Flemish and Belgian or Spanish and Catalan membership. But in the case of Brexit it is unclear what 'choice' would imply. If honouring the international legal guideline were a priority – which it is not – a choice ought to be offered in view of easing naturalisation for UK nationals in certain member states.[8] Being serious about this guideline might also mean that UK nationals in the remaining states should be offered the possibility of acquiring 'predecessor status' or the status in virtue of which they established themselves there in the first place, which might imply giving UK citizens around the EU some form of non-temporary right to stay. However, other legal positions linked to their prior Union citizenship status would not be covered, such as the anchorage of pensions to the EU system.

Occasionally, there is mention of protection of acquired rights for third country nationals; notwithstanding that, generally, nationals of countries not involved in the State succession yet residing in the territory of the successor State receive little or no attention. This category of people seems to be forgotten in most international instruments dealing with nationality and State succession: Neither the *European Convention on Nationality* nor the *Convention on Avoidance of Statelessness in Relation to State Succession* addresses the situation of nationals of third countries residing on the territory of the successor state.

Guayasén Gonzalez Marrero, who has recently completed a systematic study of international legal instruments pertaining to nationality in state succession scenarios, claims that, notwithstanding this general silence, the protection of the acquired rights of third country nationals may also be added: 'Perhaps providing a right to opt for the nationality of the newly independent State could be seen as going too far, but at least it seems desirable to preserve their status as permanent residents' (Gonzalez Marrero 2016, p. 110). One source to read in this direction is, for instance, the *Venice Declaration* of the Council of Europe that provides that where third country nationals are permanently settled on the territory, it may be possible for them to acquire the nationality of the successor state.[9] In this light we ought to read Article 16 of the *Venice Declaration*: 'The exercise of the right to choose the nationality of the predecessor state, or of one of the successor States, shall have no prejudicial consequences for those making that choice, in particular with regard to their right to residence in the successor state.'

Weighting in third country nationals into the equation concerning the right to option could mean, in the case of Brexit, that third country nationals who are family members of second country nationals in the UK are to be offered some leave to remain, even in cases not immediately covered by the domestic legislation.

5.2   SAVING CITIZENS' RIGHTS?

It is clear from the softness of the sources foreshadowed above that opportunities for freezing rights will need to be found elsewhere. The remedy venues open to post-Europeans are different from those of second country nationals in the UK since member states are continuously bound by European law. As third country nationals in the Union, British citizens resident in member states may fall within the ambit of EU law with the effect that they would be able to invoke EU general principles of law and the Charter of Fundamental Rights of the European Union in respect of their rights. They would, however, do so as third country nationals, and no longer as European citizens.[10] For many: 'Brexit presents the EU with an opportunity to clearly demonstrate the high value of European citizenship if UK nationals living in other member states can be assured that they will not lose their EU citizenship rights but rather that those rights will be 'frozen' on the day the UK formally 'leaves' the Union' (Carrera et al. 2016). How can this be done?

Residence rights can be maintained as derived from the existence of family ties with European citizens. British citizens who are family members of Union citizens are better off than those without such connections: (s)he would fall within the scope of the *Citizens Directive*, which provides for residence rights. Some EU doctrinal constructs reinforce this claim. The famous *Zhu and Chen* doctrine could impact on a member state exit scenario in which the nationality of a child be such that the child is a Union citizen and has nationality separate from that of the parents who hold the nationality of the exiting state.

The case giving name to the doctrine concerned Catherine Zhu,[11] a child born with Irish nationality *ex iure soli*, following the deliberate choice of her Chinese parents to have the child delivered in Belfast to guarantee Union citizenship be bestowed upon her. The European Court of Justice concluded that the UK could not deny the right of residence of Catherine merely because her Union citizenship had been acquired to assure residence rights for the third country national parent. The mother was recognised a right to residence in the UK on the grounds that she was primary carer to a minor Union citizen residing there.

The doctrine may have bearing on situations in which a child is born in another European member state that allows for *ius soli* at birth. In such a case, the parents of the child, as primary carer, could be granted residence rights in the Union so as not to deprive the child's rights to residence of any useful effect. Consider, for example, the case of the child who acquired Union citizenship though nationality of a member state *ex iure soli*, by birth on the territory, and the parents have UK nationality but the child does not; either because the parents are unable to pass on their nationality *ex iure sanguinis* or because the child is born on the territory of another state who does not recognise the possibility for the child to hold multiple nationalities. Such cases may derive from a combination of British and EU member state provisions. Consider, for example, the UK nationality law, according to which a person born abroad to a citizen – who acquired citizenship by descent, and is not in public service – does not acquire citizenship automatically, and is prevented from doing so through registration in the event the parent(s) have not resided at any time in the UK for three years. If these provisions are taken in a combination with the nationality provisions in Austria, Belgium, Bulgaria, Croatia, Czech Republic, France, Greece, Ireland, Italy, the Netherlands, Portugal, Romania, Slovakia, Slovenia and Spain that allow for *ius soli* acquisition combined with a variety of residence and other requirements, indeed, the Zhu doctrine may come into play.

This possibility will call for strategic decisions being made in certain families in case of Brexit. A person can enjoy certain rights attached to Union citizenship even in the case that the status as such is no longer held, even if it is merely as a flickering light of a flame that once burnt.

But how about autonomous rights to residence? Human rights treaties lay down obligations owed directly to individuals and often provide direct access for individuals to international protection mechanisms (Shaw 2014, p. 711) and remaining member states, as well as the UK, are bound by, *inter alios*, the European Convention of Human Rights, even though increasingly unpopular within certain political circles. In the event of state succession within the Union 'some rights linked to the possession of member state nationality and, therefore, to the citizenship of the Union, that are being exercised in the moment of gaining independence can be retained by certain categories of people' (Gonzalez Marrero 2016, p. 188). This would be the case also in Brexit Britain.

Is there a possible retention of residence rights to be established on the grounds of the European Convention of Human Rights and the doctrine developed by the European Court of Human Rights in the landmark *Kurić and others v. Slovenia?*[12] It could be argued that there is a strong link between the right to reside in a certain territory and the human right to private and family life as laid down in Art. 8 ECHR.[13] Most probably residence rights will be frozen.

5.2.1   The Kurić Doctrine

The case concerns some of the so-called *izbrisani* of Slovenia who had been stripped of their prior status as permanent residents, and most often also turned into stateless following the missed naturalisation in the newly independent Slovenia in the early 1990s.

When Slovenia became independent, it automatically extended citizenship to any person who had been its 'internal citizen' but not to former Socialist Federal Republic of Yugoslavia citizens holding the citizenship of one of the other republics of the former Yugoslav federation. Permanent residents did not acquire Slovenian citizenship automatically: They had a window for opting for citizenship. Those who did not apply or missed the deadline were simply erased from the registry of permanent residents. The group of *izbrisani* was created: It consisted of those who lost their previously acquired rights of residence in Slovenia (Mindus 2009).

After a long saga in the Slovenian constitutional court, the matter came before the Court in Strasbourg where, on 3 March 2009, it was ruled that 'the decisions taken by States in the immigration sphere can in some cases amount to interference with the right to respect for private and family life secured by Art. 8 § 1 of the Convention' and that 'it must be accepted that the totality of social ties between settled migrants and the community in which they are living constitute part of the concept of private life within the meaning of Art. 8' (§ 351). The applicants were nationals of both the Yugoslav republic and one of the other republics of Yugoslavia that were not Slovenia. All had permanent residence in Slovenia as citizens of the Yugoslav Republic, which gave them – in the eyes of Strasbourg – 'a stronger residence status than long-term migrants.' The punch line of *Kurić* is that 'once you have lawfully established residency, you keep the rights of residence, even if the legal status of either your home State or your host State changes and, as a result of this change, your new nationality status alone would no longer give you a right to residence' (Vidmar 2013, p. 28).

Although the facts in *Kurić* and Brexit differ,[14] the premise remains: Residency was lawfully established prior to change in legal status and, if the UK will proceed with withdrawal from the EU, that right of residence will be kept, even if the nationality status alone would no longer give a right of residence. Regardless of whether or not the person concerned resides in EU territory upon independence, by virtue of the *Kurić* doctrine, the residence status will be frozen. However, 'the further development of that status after independence – defrosting of the residence status – will certainly be different if the residence has been frozen in the territory of a member state or in the territory of the exited state' (Gonzalez Marrero 2016, p. 208). The *Kurić* formula would 'cement' the existing residence rights, but would not extend the applicability of European law to the territories exiting the EU.

The implications for second country nationals in the UK and for British citizens in the Union will be different. The freezing of rights for the first category will depend, once exit is effected, exclusively on domestic law's reading of the boundaries imposed by international law. Generally, there will be issues raised in relation to the enforcement in the UK of the withdrawal treaty. The protection offered by the *Kurić* formula to the second group has limitations. Its protection is territorially restricted. It only guarantees those rights attached to the residence status as far as the person concerned does not move to another member state. Therefore, being granted the status of long-term resident third country national is to be preferred to merely relying on the *Kurić* formula: Long-term resident third country nationals are not chained to one member state.[15] They exercise freedom of movement akin to that of Union citizens as they acquire a right to reside in member states other than the one that granted the status.

5.2.2   Residence Rights in the EU

Two are the practical implications for UK nationals residing in member states with no other nationality to fall back on. First, due to the *Kurić* doctrine, the residence within the EU of nationals from the exited state is deemed to be legal. Even in the event of a non-negotiated cataclysmic withdrawal member states would not be allowed to consider UK nationals illegal migrants.

Second, British citizens around the Union would do well to have their position regularised as long-term resident third country nationals. Member states are not required to, but may consider facilitate the regularisation of British nationals as long-term resident third country nationals. Both the *Citizens directive* and the *Third country nationals long-term residence directive* refer to the same quantitative (five years) and qualitative (continuous residence) requirements regarding the period of residence necessary to acquire permanent residence or long-term residence status. The second country national has in practice already met the requirement to be granted a long-term residence permit as a third country national. A first policy can thus be suggested: Unless the requirements have ceased to be met, the change of status from Union citizen with right of residence to third country national with a long-term residence permit ought to be granted automatically to British citizens who have already acquired the right to permanent residence in the host member state. Basically, Brits having lived in a member state for five years or more can stay. A stronger version of this policy suggestion has been made by scholars who have recently suggested that 'a fairly modest legislative change to the *Long-term residence directive* that would mitigate the predicament of UK citizens could be the granting of Long-term resident status to mobile UK citizens, irrespective of whether they have met the continuous residence and/or other LTRD requirements' (Ziegler 2016).

Many countries require third country nationals to comply with integration requirements before becoming long-term residents, including the UK. Integration tests, that are mentioned in the *Third country national long-term residence directive* but not in the *Citizens directive*, may be a hinder for freshly minted third country nationals with British passports, probably still European in colour, who may be subjected to such tests. Another policy suggestion could be to ease, or waive, the requirement of integration tests (and/or make sure these tests are not unreasonably strict or costly) so as to facilitate the makeover from second country national to third country national.

Those having lived in the country less than five years could also be granted leave to stay: Former Union citizens living in member states since less than five years would be able to make a claim in favour of freezing rights in the process of being acquired; since the *Kurić* doctrine would count to protect residence rights to be taken into account for a future application for status as long-term third country national.

Residence rights will be recognised for post-Europeans in the Union. Perhaps they will be harder to enforce for second country nationals in the UK, but also their residence rights have chances of being frozen. According to Richard Gordon and Rowena Mofatt, for instance, there are two strands of case law of relevance in seeking remedy for the 'vested rights' of second country nationals: The first, relating to vested rights and the second relating to fairness and, in particular, the doctrine of substantive legitimate expectation. The question of vested rights has been explored in the context of the Immigration Rules in the case of *Odelola v. Secretary of State for the Home Department*. European citizens would be in a far stronger position to invoke the presumption against retrospectivity in the event that a UK withdrawal from the EU altered or removed their existing free movement rights enjoyed in the UK. But this presumption against retrospectivity is valid only 'in absence of express statutory language to the contrary' (Gordon and Mofatt 2016). According to the same source, 'it is considered likely that the common law would be astute enough to protect the pre-existing interests of EU citizens in the UK in the event of a UK withdrawal' (Gordon and Mofatt 2016).

In sum, British citizens may thus be granted leave to stay in the Union. By the same token, we cannot exclude that second country nationals could see their residence rights frozen also in the UK.

5.3   THE WRONG SAVIOUR?

We have shown that there are ways to secure 'acquired residence rights' by European citizens living in the UK and British nationals living elsewhere in the Union, by relying on the *Kurić* doctrine. Residence rights for all other categories than family members of Union citizens and primary carers of minor Union citizens resident in the EU cannot be upheld on the basis of European law. The rights of residence linked to free movement – a most celebrated *acquis* and beloved by many mobile Union citizens – will not fall prey to the idiosyncrasies of the electorate in a member state, nor held hostage by static citizens as many fear. They will be saved, but not by the workings of the *acquis*. The most cherished entitlements of Europeans will need to be saved by international law.

As far as the *content* of Union citizenship is concerned, (some) rights may be frozen, but the rights that may be frozen are not rights of the kind that would make Union citizenship a supranational legal status. Indeed, we are dealing with rights, the *ratio personae* of which does not coincide with that of Union citizenship. Residence rights as, in general, freedom of movement are, *repetita juvant*, not pertaining exclusively to the citizens of the Union. Their personal scope is both over- and under-inclusive in relation to the category of Union citizens. Many have long been unconvinced by their supposed supranational character. In fact, freedom of movement is not recognised unconditionally to Union citizens (as underscored by Case C-333/13 *Dano* EU:C:2014:2358) and a number of third country nationals are covered by the *acquis* in relation to freedom of movement. Third country nationals holding a valid residence permit or visa have the right to move freely within the Schengen area for up to three months within a six-month period. The rights in relation to taking up residence for a period exceeding three months in another member state is covered by specific legal instruments, depending on their status, and subject to conditions in national legislation (e.g. blue card, intracorporate tranfers, long-term residents, researchers, students).

Legal positions founded on the 'mutual commitment to open their respective bodies politic to other European citizens and to construct a new form (...) of political allegiance on a European scale' – to use the phrasing of Poaires Maduro in the *Rottman* case – are rightly called 'supranational.' Such supranational rights associated with Union citizenship – first and foremost, the right to vote and stand in elections in the European Parliament and the right to the Citizens' initiative – will be lost with the status. Those whose nationality is no longer linked to a member state, due to the withdrawal of that State, lose their 'fundamental status' as previously conceived. They cannot invoke *civis europaeus sum*. The question thus arises: Is it lawful for a member state to strip their own nationals of Union citizenship? This is a question regarding the extension, not the intension of membership in the EU. So let us move on to investigate this second dimension of citizenship of the Union in the next chapter.

NOTES

1. For an explanation of why the so-called precedents are not relevant, see Chapter 4.
2. Some analogies are clearly fallacious: Consider, for example, the parallel drawn between Union citizenship and the status of commonwealth citizen, a status common to all kinds of British nationality statuses and citizens of commonwealth countries. The acquisition and loss of this status is a matter to be regulated by the Commonwealth. Historically speaking, the UK allowed people from territories gaining independence to maintain the overarching subjecthood to the Commonwealth, since the latter defines *its* own citizens. While this analogy is fit to test the theory of internal enlargement for cases such as Scotland, Flanders and Catalonia, it has no traction in Brexit since the UK never exited the Commonwealth.
3. See, e.g. Douglas-Scott 2016. Some evidence suggests that private rights under municipal law such as property and contractual rights may be frozen according to customary international law. Doctrine is divided when it comes to automatic accession to Human Rights Treaties in case of state succession. But even if automatic accession did take place it would not help protecting the 'special rights' of EU citizens.
4. Note verbale of the Delegation of the EU to the UN 19 September 2012, § A$_4$.
5. Reference re Secession of Quebec, [1998] 2 *S.C.R.* 217.

6. See International Law Commission, *Articles of Nationality of Natural Persons in Relation to the Succession of States (with Commentaries)*, 3 April 1999, Supplement No. 10 (A/54/10).

7. *Ibidem*, at 30.

8. Reference is to those bound by the *European Convention on Nationality*, namely Austria, Bulgaria, Czeck Republic, Denmark, Finland, Germany, Hungary, the Netherlands, Portugal, Romania, Slovakia and Sweden. Besides the many reservations made to European Convention on Nationality, it might also be a dubious solution for some of these countries for internal reasons: for example, Austria enforces a ban on multiple nationalities; Sweden already has a comparatively easy naturalisation process; Denmark imposes integrations tests, etc.

9. *Declaration on the Consequences of State Succession for the Nationality of Natural Persons (and Commentary)*, reproduced in Council of Europe, European Commission for Democracy though Law, 'Consequences of State Succession for the Nationality' CDL-INF (97).

10. Some have even pointed out that if UK citizens were non-EU citizens (third-country nationals), they could apply for asylum in the EU (and vice versa). This prospect, however, seems improbable. A more probable effect is that it will be harder also for UK to obtain extradiction from EU member states. The recent *Petruhhin* ruling (Case C-182/15 ECLI:EU: C:2016:630) takes a step towards EU *exclusive* competence over extradition treaties with non-EU countries. It may become unlawful to extradict to the UK; there are several challenges in Ireland to the execution of British European arrest warrants following the Brexit vote.

11. Case C-20/02 *Zhu and Chen* (2004) ECR I-09951.

12. Application No. 26828/06, 26 June 2012 *Kuric v Slovenia*.

13. The connection between Art. 8 ECHR and EU law has been stressed previously: See Wiesbrock 2009 at 199 – in relation to residence rights of third country nationals who are family members of European citizens. Then again, the directive on permanent residence rights for EU citizens also regulates the residence rights of their family members (See *Directive* 2004/58/EC).

14. There is, nonetheless, a similarity in circumstances between the cases insofar as the UK may be tempted to deny continued rights to residency to a number of citizens with non-UK member state nationality, similarly to how Slovenia denied it to those who had nationality of other states emerging from the break-up of Yugoslavia who however had, at the time of the former federation, established their permanent residency in Slovenia, just like second country nationals enjoy Treaty rights on UK soil.

15. See Council Directive 2003/109/EC of 25 November 2003 concerning the status of third-country nationals who are long-term residents: After five years of continuous residence (Article 4 LTRD) and subject to satisfying additional criteria, LTRs acquire the right to reside in the territory of member States other than the one which granted them the long-term residence status (Article 14(1) LTRD).

REFERENCES

Carrera, S., E. Guild, and N. Chun Luk. (2016) 'What Does Brexit Mean for the EU's Area of Freedom, Security and Justice?', *CEPS,* July 2016, available at https://www.ceps.eu/publications/what-does-brexit-mean-eu%E2%80%99s-area-freedom-security-and-justice (last accessed 30 October 2016).

Closa, C. (ed.) (2014) *Troubled Membership: Dealing with Secession from a Member State and Withdrawal from the Union,* RSCAS 2014/91. RSCAS Publications, Fiesole.

Douglas-Scott, S. (2016) 'What Happens to Acquired Rights in the Event of Brexit?', U.K. Const. L. Blog (16th May 2016), available at https://ukconsti tutionallaw.org/2016/05/16/sionaidh-douglas-scott-what-happens-to-acquired-rights-in-the-event-of-a-brexit/ (last accessed 30 October 2016).

Gonzalez Marrero, G. (2016) *Civis Europaeus Sum? Consequences with Regard to Nationality Law and EU Citizenship Status of the Independence of a Devolved Part of an EU Member State,* Nijmegen: Wolf Legal Publishers.

Gordon, R., and R. Mofatt (2016) *Brexit: The Immediate Legal Consequences,* Report for The Constitution Society, available at http://www.consoc.org.uk/wp-con tent/uploads/2016/05/Brexit-PDF.pdf (last accessed 30 October 2016).

Kochenov, D. (2016) 'Brexit and the Argentinianisation of British Citizenship: Taking Care Not To Overstay Your 90 Days in Rome, Amsterdam or Paris', *VerfBlog,* 24 June 2016, available at http://verfassungsblog.de/brexit-and-the-argentinisation-of-british-citizenship-taking-care-not-to-overstay-your-90-days-in-rome-amsterdam-or-paris/ (last accessed 30 October 2016).

Mindus, P. (2009) 'The Contemporary Debate on Citizenship. Some Remarks on the Erased of Slovenia', 9 *Revus European Constitutionality Review* 29–44. Slovenian version transl. by Jernej Ogrin.

Shaw, M. (2014) *International Law,* 7th ed., Cambridge: CUP.

Vidmar, J. (2013) 'The Scottish Independence Referendum in an International Context', 51 *Canadian Yearbook of International Law* 259–288.

Wiesbrock, A. (2009) *Legal Migration to the European Union: Ten Years After Tampere,* Maastricht: Wolf.

Ziegler, R., *UK Citizens as Former EU? Citizens: Predicament and Remedies*, EUDO Forum Debates 'Freedom of Movement Under Attack: Is it Worth Defending as the Core of EU Citizenship?, available at http://eudo-citizen ship.eu/commentaries/citizenship-forum/citizenship-forum-cat/1586-free dom-of-movement-under-attack-is-it-worth-defending-as-the-core-of-eu-citi zenship?showall=&start=12 (last accessed 12 November 2016).

CHAPTER 6

Who Gets to Withdraw the Status?

Abstract This chapter determines the extension of Union citizenship by asking: Who gets to withdraw the status of Union citizenship? It is a complex and debated issue. The various options are presented and the anticipated consequences for both the UK and EU states are fleshed out. Venues for challenging the loss of status are also discussed. The chapter discusses limits to what the UK can do to protect itself against abuse of multiple citizenship and what member states are allowed to do to UK citizens resident in their territories. The key finding is that while member states are in principle free to revoke the status of Union citizen, former member states are not unbounded in stripping Union citizens of their acquired territorial rights.

Keywords European citizenship · Brexit · Freedom of movement · Right of residence · EU law · Migration law · International law · Political rights · Citizens' initiative

6.1 Who Gets to Withdraw Union Citizenship?

This chapter explores the extension of Union citizenship, by asking who determines loss of Union citizenship. Can member states impose involuntary loss of EU citizenship? What are the limits to state discretion in this area? What material consequences may follow from such limits?

© The Author(s) 2017
P. Mindus, *European Citizenship after Brexit*, Palgrave Studies
in European Union Politics, DOI 10.1007/978-3-319-51774-2_6

It was long supposed that the only way to lose European citizenship for a European citizen was by losing member state nationality. Already the Resolution on the draft Treaty establishing the EU from 14 February 1984, stressed that European citizenship 'may not be (...) forfeited (...) independently of nationality of a member state.'[1] With Brexit the nationality of the former member state is not lost, but Union citizenship would be. So Brexit proves that there is another way to lose 'the fundamental status': *Ex lege* automatic loss due to the exiting of a member state. Indirectly, Article 50 adds a ground for loss of Union citizenship. This ground for loss finds its mirror image in the acquisition of Union citizenship *ex lege* for states acceding to the Union according to Article 49 TFEU. The argument, in keeping with traditional theories of statehood, is that any mutation to the legal status of territory can thus naturally be expected to generate effects for the citizenship status of (at least some) inhabitants.

With Brexit, we are witnessing a form of involuntary loss[2] of citizenship *en masse, ex lege*, imposed on EU citizens of British nationality that, however, does not create statelessness and is likely to be tolerated under public international law. Involuntary here indicates the modality of loss, not the will of the status holder. *Legally*, the loss of citizenship is involuntary insofar as it is not a case of (individual) renunciation. In the case of Brexit one may also make the *political* claim that it is involuntary because 48% expressed their will to remain European citizens; certain territories voted massively in favour of staying and the UK citizens residing abroad were disenfranchised, even though they were among the most affected.[3] Can such an involuntary loss be unilaterally imposed by an exiting state? If so, what consequences follow in the current legal setting? No Treaty provision explicitly deals with the consequences of loss of Union citizenship. Any consequences would need to be found in non-primary sources.

At first sight, whether involuntary loss can be imposed by the state that exits seems very simple to answer. Even though access to the status is, formally, regulated by the Treatises, Union citizenship is not an autonomous status. The choice of using mere lexical reference to member state nationality laws in Article 20 TFEU leaves the *Herren der Verträge* (Masters of the Treaties), in principle, free to determine such criteria. This has, among other things, permitted member states aiming to deprive of rights certain minority groups among their citizens to engage in the inelegant practice of bringing unilateral declarations on the meaning of nationality for the purposes of EU law.[4]

All in all, Article 20 TFEU leaves little doubt about who owns the competence: 'Every person holding the nationality of a member state shall be a citizen of the Union. Citizenship of the Union shall be additional to and not replace national citizenship.' It is confirmed by the wording of the declaration annexed to the Maastricht Treaty on the nationality of member states: 'The question whether an individual possesses the nationality of the Member state shall be settled *solely* by reference to the national law of the Member State concerned.'[5] In this context, it is worth recalling the doubts of the Danes, expressed during the summit in Edinburgh, who feared that European citizenship would substitute their own *infødsret*. Only after many specifications as to the adjunctive character of the new status, did Denmark ratify the Treaty of Maastricht following a second referendum (Howarth 1994).

The rule governing the allocation of competence in the area of nationality law is entrenched in international law and recently codified in the Article 3(1) European Convention on Nationality: 'Each State shall determine under its own law who are its nationals.' Member states share this view too. Suffice to say that the German constitutional court, in its *Lissabon Urteil* from 2009, expressed the point as follows: 'In view of the elaboration of the rights of the citizens of the Union, the German state people (*Staatsvolk*) retains its existence as long as the citizenship of the Union does not replace the citizenships of the Member States or is superimposed on it.'[6]

Member states own the competence to define criteria for acquisition and loss of their own nationality. Nationality of a member state is a necessary criterion for acquisition of EU citizenship. This determines the *derivative* nature of EU citizenship that confers upon it the quality of a complementary status, different from dual citizenship status common in federal states.[7] Unclearness hovers above the construct and it allows indirect influence of member states on the definition of *who* counts a Union citizens. For some, EU law and domestic law would even constitute competing norms (e.g. Evans 1991). As mentioned in Chapter 2, a famous paradox is that as a result of the Spanish option right for the children of former Spanish nationals born in Spain (Art. 20 of the Spanish Civil Code), Fidel Castro himself could immediately opt for European citizenship without moving from Havana (De Groot 2004, p. 7).

One might be tempted to conclude that the remedial solutions for avoiding the loss of status for the category of British nationals living in other member states are therefore nil: Vain would be the attempt to domesticate the sovereign power to exclude of an exiting member state.

The short answer to the question put in the title of this section is member states, but a more nuanced answer adds *granu salis*. The question whether an individual possesses the nationality of the member state is no longer settled *solely* by reference to the national law. The famous declaration attached to the Maastricht Treaty on 'nationality' was removed from the annex of the TEU after entry into force of the Lisbon Treaty. There are limits to the ability of member states to impose involuntary loss of citizenship entailing curtailment of previously enjoyed rights. Supranational scrutiny of state discretion in this area is increasing.

6.2   LIMITS OF PUBLIC INTERNATIONAL LAW

A set of international norms pertains to the withdrawing of *status civitatis* as such. The power of states to determine its members is not unfettered. The decision to revoke nationality finds its limits in international norms in the form of treaties or customary law.[8] Leading principles on loss of nationality can be found in the Articles 5–9 of the 1961 *Convention on the Reduction of Statelessness* and as well as the 1997 *European Convention on Nationality*. However, such instruments would not apply since Brexit would not cause statelessness. So what other sources are there?

Article 15 of the Universal Declaration on Human Rights states that 'everyone has the right to a nationality,' which may not be withdrawn arbitrarily. Although the Universal Declaration is not a binding instrument, the forbiddance of arbitrary deprivation is repeated in other treatises and instruments. 'Deprivation,' which domestically is an act of the administration, in this setting covers *ex lege loss* of nationality.[9] An example of such an arbitrary loss is, for example, a retroactive restriction of a ground for acquisition.[10]

A first practical implication follows from here. The UK cannot, lest it violates international law, retroactively deprive second country nationals who have naturalised in the UK of their current status were it somehow to push for expulsion of 'non-Brits' altogether; nor can the UK retroactively deprive of British nationality citizens who, having the citizenship by birth of another EU member state, also naturalised in the UK. This is a first limit to the possibilities of the exiting state to protect itself against instrumental use of multiple citizenship.

Now all provisions on loss of citizenship need to be read in the light of the general principle of the UNDHR banning arbitrary deprivation. The Universal Declaration does not specify the exact circumstances under which one would have to conclude that there is an arbitrary withdrawal (Marescaux 1984) but some general principles follow from this obligation to avoid *arbitrariness.*[11] These principles have to be observed not only if the loss or deprivation would cause statelessness, but in all cases where a person would be stripped of a citizenship. The Brexit loss provision would need to obey these principles.

An intriguing issue is whether the loss of Union citizenship entailed by Brexit might demonstrate arbitrary features in its being unchallengeable. The application of loss provisions must be possible to challenge in court, but in this scenario, it is unclear whether the principle would imply letting British citizens challenge the loss provision before an English court, before courts in member states where they are residing, or before the European Court of Justice. As we shall see there is a quite limited possibility that the European Court of Justice might be involved. Were this the case, the Brexit loss provision would comply with international law requirement on being challengeable. While it seems likely that some rights associated with Union citizenship could be upheld if deprivation of these was challenged, it is less clear if loss of the status as such could be challenged, let alone if it could be frozen for the British citizens concerned.

6.3   EU Law Limits to State Discretion

At first the Brexit case of loss of Union citizenship does not seem to fall within the remit of European law precisely because it would occur simultaneously to the UK's withdrawal, but appearances deceive. The jurisprudence of the European Court of Justice has imposed certain limitations on the autonomous powers of the member States to determine issues relating to the acquisition and loss of nationality. Generally speaking, member states need to pay 'due regard to Community law.' This has been the *obiter dictum* since the European Court of Justice started to express itself on the matter in the early Nineties, with the case of the Argentinian dentist *Micheletti.*[12]

On that occasion, the European Court of Justice concluded that:

under international law, it is for each Member State, having *due regard to Community law,* to lay down the conditions for the acquisition and loss of nationality. However, it is not permissible for the legislation of a Member State to restrict the effects of the grant of the nationality of another Member State by imposing an additional condition for recognition of that nationality with a view to the exercise of the fundamental freedoms provided for in the Treaty.[13]

Besides public international law, member states are to respect general principles of European law that applies to matters of loss of Union citizenship, including the principle of proportionality – that has attracted much interest in the wake of *Rottman* – but also the principle of equal treatment, the principle of protection of legitimate expectations and the principle of sincere cooperation (*Gemeinschaftstraue*).

In *Rottman*, the European Court of Justice acknowledged that member states may legitimise the revocation of nationality and its consequences for the status of European citizens for the protection of their special relationship with their nationals, based on 'solidarity and good faith, and the reciprocity of rights and duties, which forms the bedrock of the bond of nationality.'[14] Such legitimate interest is, however, subject to the test of proportionality and other limits. The European Court of Justice left it up to the national court to decide whether it would be proportional to withdraw German nationality. Even after *Rottman* it is compatible with European law to deprive naturalised of citizenship in case of fraud – which is also consistent with international law – but member states:

> must not solely adhere to this principle of proper administration in accordance with their own internal (administrative law), where exclusively national points of view will be dealt with (...); but then a second proportionality test must be applied regarding this loss of the fundamental status of Union citizen. That element can, of course, already be included in the proportionality test by national law, but to the extent that it is not the case, it must be examined separately. (Jessurun d'Oliveira 2011, p. 8)

For completing the proportionality test the European Court of Justice provides a number of criteria to take into consideration: The position of family members who might lose rights of residence; the seriousness of the fraud involved; time elapsed between naturalisation and deprivation; if the person may recover prior nationality. It has been stressed that the principle of proportionality ought to be paramount to all decisions on loss, including those where loss occurs automatically (*ex lege*). Since *Rottman*, it is clear that member states are subjected to the general principles of European law in matters such as loss of Union citizenship.

Nationality law belongs to the *domaine réservé* but domestic choices are not neutral *vis-à-vis* Union citizenship. There may be incentives for the UK to adopt or modify domestic provisions in a way, however, that would need to pay 'due regard' to European law.[15]

6.3.1 Resisting Temptation

An exiting member state has a strong interest to curb opportunities to fool its intention to exit. A palatable way of doing so is to retain nationality of the exiting state *and* EU citizenship: By having, or acquiring, multiple citizenship, by birth or by naturalisation, in the exiting state and in other member states that do not enforce a ban on multiple nationalities. Multiple nationalities may be the answer for many wishing to retain both residence rights in the UK and free movement in the Union. This is especially the case in Northern Ireland, which already has half a million Irish passport holders. Many people in the UK are Irish citizens by descent from parents or grandparents born in Northern Ireland or the Republic of Ireland. In some cases, in order to establish their citizenship, they will first need to enter their names on the register of foreign births. But for many people asserting their Irish citizenship, which has been dormant is simply a matter of applying for an Irish passport (Dzankic 2016).

After Brexit, UK residents with Irish and British citizenship will still be both UK and EU citizens. 'In a future where the UK is proposing to close its borders to EU nationals, this issue [of double citizenship of many Irish] may become very controversial, as EU nationals are unlikely to benefit from similar 'dual nationalities' in large numbers (...) following a full Brexit' (De Mars et al. 2016). Unsurprisingly, the House of Lords European Union Committee launched an inquiry into UK-Irish relations on 1st of September 2016. Under the banner of taking back control, the UK may be spurred to restrict pervasive (ab)use of multiple citizenships and/or to tolerate it only in some cases.

While any exiting State may have a strong incentive to penalise instrumental naturalisation and abuse of multiple citizenships, the case of the UK is particularly interesting since it has a tradition of tolerance in this regard. Following the 1948 British Nationality Act, multiple nationalities have been tolerated in the UK system: Since 1 January 1949 the voluntary acquisition of a foreign nationality did not automatically cause the loss of British nationality. It was in principle possible for an individual to retain British nationality, combined with citizenship of the Commonwealth and/or foreign nationality. British decolonisation allowed for multiple citizenships more often than not, with the exception of not promoting it systematically for territories claiming independence. If the country stays on its path, it will allow multiple citizenship, permitting some people to effectively be British and European citizens at the same time.

Generally, in former British territories that achieved independence, the provisions dealing with the consequences for nationality had a recurring theme: The person who became a national of the newly independent State under its initial laws, would cease on that day to be a British citizen, with exceptions based on a connection with the UK or remaining British colonies (Fransman 2011, p. 607). Similar provisions can be found in the independence acts of the following British colonies: Uganda, Kenya, Gambia, Botswana, Lesotho, Malta, Trinidad & Tobago, Barbados, Guyana, Jamaica and Cyprus. If we look at nationality provisions in the Independence acts of countries such as the commonwealth country Nigeria, Ghana, the Malayan federation, Zambia or Malawi we recognise the same pattern: The question of who kept British nationality largely depended on whether one would acquire nationality of the newly independent state.

In keeping with this tradition, the UK ought not to oppose retaining of European citizenship on the part of the population that has 'obvious ties' to the EU.[16] Were British citizens having 'obvious ties' to the EU somehow offered to maintain their prior status as EU citizens, the UK would need to break with its traditional tolerance in order to oppose it. The UK is not well-equipped to prevent instrumental use of multiple citizenships, but it still has some options that it might be tempted to use.

Given the focus on migration in the debate leading up to the referendum, an incentive for the UK could also be to harden its domestic immigration law, or seek to pick and choose which second country nationals it is willing to admit to residency or to naturalisation. This can be done by reforming nationality or immigration law, but there are more subtle ways of achieving this: For example, by sharpening requirements in citizenship tests[17] to make naturalisation a harder option for low skilled EU migrants, or by raising fees for requiring indefinite leave to remain or for naturalising in the UK. Currently fees are very high and rising and it is unclear what costs for applicants we would be dealing with.

Conversely, the exiting member state may also choose to penalise instrumental naturalisation by its own nationals living in other member states. One option might be to re-introduce additional criteria, such as the requirement of 'a genuine link'[18] to strengthen one's claim of having British citizenship; an option fully in line with international law. This option may lead to stripping of some rights but not of *status civitatis* as such since the UK does not impose lapse of citizenship because of residence abroad. However, it cannot be excluded that a *revirement* towards the genuine link doctrine of an exiting member state may implicate statelessness in cases in which the member state provides for loss of citizenship for those citizens who permanently reside in another state and who do not have another nationality to rely on. In ten member states citizens may lose nationality due to continuous residence abroad.[19] Another option for penalising instrumental naturalisation of British citizens abroad would be making life difficult for UK nationals wishing to renounce to their original citizenship in order to naturalise in states of the Union that enforce a ban on dual nationality,[20] for example, by raising fees and making it economically costly to renounce.

These incentives, and many others, would need to be resisted. During the two-year *interregnum* following an invocation of Article 50, the exiting member state would need to observe the limits imposed by European law on its ability to modify its own provisions on nationality and migration. Were the UK to modify its policy in ways incompatible with European law, it could be subjected to infringement procedure by the Commission and judicial review by the European Court of Justice. The policy adopted under the *interregnum* would also have practical implications once the UK has effectuated the exit from the Union.

6.3.2 Consequences for the UK

By paying attention to the doctrinal limits of European law to state discretion in this policy area, the anticipated consequences for the UK are that, during the *interregnum* phase, European law would still hold and it could possibly have an *après-coup* effect on the formulation of domestic nationality law. Modifications to policies even within the *domaine réservé* may come to be scrutinised by the European Court of Justice.

In particular, if the UK passes reforms to its domestic nationality law, these would be subjected to judicial review by the European Court of Justice. The UK would be prevented from hardening its domestic nationality law with the aim to punish instrumental acquisition of multiple nationalities. More precisely, the UK cannot pass domestic nationality provisions easing naturalisation only for some EU citizens: It would violate the principle of equality or non-discrimination. The UK would also be prevented from passing domestic nationality provisions having the effect of barring, or rendering more difficult or overly onerous, naturalisation of second country nationals, since such a policy would violate the principle of legitimate expectations. It is not impossible that making applications for indefinite leave to remain harder would also be held to be at odds with this general principle of European law.

Furthermore, the UK would be prevented from fighting instrumental naturalisation of its own nationals. It could not strip instrumental naturalisers of their British nationality and/or residence rights. It could be hard to prevent double residence for citizens with multiple nationalities. The UK might favour a return to the genuine link doctrine, developed by the *Nottebohm*-jurisprudence prevailing in international law, which considers citizenship to be 'a social fact of attachment'[21] to claim that, if the person has his/her habitual residence or other key interests in the UK, the 'effective nationality' is the British membership, and not the nationality of the member state the person also is a member of. European law, however, prevents the UK from requiring such citizens to have a 'genuine link' with it. Finally, the UK would probably not be allowed to raise fees in any significant way for British nationals wishing to renounce nationality with the purpose of becoming naturalised in other parts of the Union.

In general terms, it would be detrimental to negotiations to harden the UK nationality laws and/or immigration laws. It should not be excluded that it would be favourable to negotiations to move in the opposite direction, for example, providing for automatic transformation of permanent residence into indefinite leave to remain, allowing second country nationals to naturalise without being subjected to citizenship tests or disproportionate fees. No such political will has been expressed.

6.3.3   *Consequences for Member States*

The policies listed above would fall within the remit of European law, allowing the European Court of Justice to scrutinise their legitimacy as long as the negotiations would last. The doctrinal limits in European law and their anticipated consequences for member states *vis-à-vis* UK nationals are also worthy of attention. Member states are hindered from a series of other actions that may tempt or that have already been suggested. In particular, there are limits to what member states can do to both assist and deter British citizens from continuing living in the Union and eventually naturalising there. Member states cannot 'punish' British citizens: Some countries having many nationals resident in the UK and that have been particularly targeted in the Brexit debate may not, for instance, render family reunification for British citizens harder, since it would violate the principle of legitimate expectations. Perhaps, it would also be advisable to let British citizens naturalise in Spain without enforcing the ban on dual nationality; or let them naturalise regardless of performance in integration tests in countries requiring these.

Academics have suggested naturalising Brits to save their rights (Kochenov 2016; Steinbeis 2016). Similar ideas have been voiced by senior politicians. Matteo Renzi hinted that British students might be offered naturalisation in Italy. German Vice-Chancellor Sigmar Gabriel said the remaining members should not 'pull up the drawbridge' for young Britons, and Germany should consider offering dual nationality to young British citizens.[22] Such suggestions may be at odds with EU law. While individual naturalisation cases would fall within the competences of member states, it has become increasingly clear that were a member state to singlehandedly offer such *en masse* naturalisation it would challenge the principle of sincere cooperation. It is worth recalling that the Commission's DG Justice proceeded to infringement proceedings against Malta in relation to the Individual investor program initiated in 2013, which had been criticised by the European Parliament. It was the first time that a member state's nationality law was subjected to substantial amendment following an infringement proceeding. It has been pointed out both in literature (already in Kotalakidis 2000) and in court that the principle of sincere cooperation constitutes a limit to the exercise of state discretion, specifically in relation to what would be a mass naturalisation. If such naturalisation is to be an option, it requires the assent of the remaining 26 States. The Advocate General Poiares Maduro stated that provisions of primary Community legislation and the general principles of community law could restrict the legislative power of member states in the sphere of nationality: 'Thus, mention has been made (...) of the Community principle of sincere cooperation laid down in Article 10 EC, which could be affected if a member state were to carry out, without consulting the Commission or its partners, an unjustified mass naturalisation of nationals of non-member states.'[23]

Finally, another possible doctrinal limit of EU law is the requirement to offer time to re-lapse. After *Rottman*, citizens need to have a chance, before their newly acquired member state nationality may be revoked, to apply for the re-acquisition of their old nationality. Commentators have ventured a reasonable timeframe would be 'a few years.' It is questionable if the Court would accept immediately effective deprivation. In the case of exit from the Union, this may be a doctrinal construct relevant to cover cases of second country nationals who naturalised in the exiting State but now wish to recover their original citizenship so as not to lose Union citizenship. Given the traditional tolerance of multiple citizenship in the UK, nonetheless, this is unlikely to constitute an impediment in practice since naturalisers never were requested to renounce their prior status.

There are limits to what States can do, even within their *domaine réservé* that may prove to have repercussions on domestic legislation insofar as it is not overturned after exit. The limits stemming from European law are therefore significant, even though limited in time. To be sure, the European Court of Justice remains a powerful player throughout the negotiation phase. Perhaps later also were the European Court of Justice selected as conflict resolution mechanism in the withdrawal treaty. Yet it is far from clear that general principles of European law would be successfully invoked before UK courts. Some have rightly stressed that the introduction of Union citizenship places an important limit on the power of member state to deprive an individual of his or her nationality (Hall 1995, 1996, 2001). However it remains to be seen if limits to State discretion could offset domestic initiatives when at stake is the power of a former member state to deprive its own nationals of their Union citizenship.

6.4   To Challenge Loss of Status

For some: 'there is room for decoupling the concepts of nationality and Union citizenship: By maintaining Union citizenship in the case of loss of Member state nationality. (...) If the EU sees Union Citizenship as a fundamental status for the peoples of Europe, then the EU can determine that certain groups of people who lose their member state nationality will nonetheless remain Union citizens.' (Jessurun d'Oliveira 2011, p. 13)

Leaving aside the risk of introducing an unjustified distinction between cases of loss and cases of acquisition, it is a fact that there have been voices in favour of decoupling Union citizenship from member state nationality since the inception of the status. Normatively, it has long been argued that not only citizens of member states should be equipped with EU citizenship but also third country nationals who have established themselves in the Union (already in Føllesdal 1993). The political legitimacy of such a de-coupling would rely on the fact that, for the first time in the history of integration, Union citizens, who had automatically acquired their supranational citizenship with the Treaty of Maastricht, raised their political voice to state that they want to *remain* European citizens. European citizenship did not formally exist at the time of the 1975 UK referendum on EU membership, and citizens voting in the EU accession referendums in the context of the 2004 enlargements were not European citizens beforehand.

Leaving aside the political unlikelihood and the legal cumbersomeness of re-drafting primary EU legislation for a formal decoupling, little help for those advocating decoupling is to be found in international sources dealing with federal citizenship structures in the event of succession.[24] Likewise – *pace* some suggestions recently made[25] – the genuine substance doctrine from *Ruiz Zambrano*,[26] that overcomes the traditional requirement that Union citizenship be activated by border-crossing, would not allow decoupling: The doctrine, at odds with the reverse discrimination of static citizens (Tryfonidou 2008), has been much watered down. It is exceptional[27] and the *ratio decidendi* is to be interpreted strictly.[28] It cannot serve as a basis for claims made by first country nationals, that is, nationals who have not made use of the freedom of movement, against the loss of status.

A more interesting candidate is the consequential reasoning in *Rottman* that specifically deals with loss of Union citizenship. In this case of great constitutional importance, the European Court of Justice concluded that 'a citizen of the Union who is faced with a decision withdrawing his [citizenship], and placing him (...) in a position capable of causing him to lose the status conferred by Article 17 EC [Article 20 TFEU] and the rights attaching thereto falls, *by reason of its nature and its consequences*, within the ambit of European Union law.'[29] The reason why this case may carry precedential value is that the case focuses on loss of Union citizenship: The European Court of Justice decided that Janko Rottmann could, unlike Ms. Kaur,[30] rely on his rights as a European citizen. Comparing the situation of Mr. Rottmann with that of Ms. Kaur, the denial of access to nationality would not constitute a problem, but the very fact that Rottmann once had the status of Union citizen, which he lost, was crucial in order to fall within the scope of European law. The *Rottman* doctrine is applicable not only to cases of deprivation when a fraud is discovered and the statelessness is the result, but also in other cases of deprivation, even if no statelessness is caused but the EU citizenship could be lost.[31]

The *Rottman* judgement points to a re-ordering of the relationship between member states' nationality and Union citizenship in favour of the latter. Gareth Davis, for one, speaks of abandonment of the hierarchy of the two concepts in favour of 'citizenship pluralism' (Davis 2011). Observers of the successive jurisprudence by the Court of Justice on Union citizenship were not surprised to discover the activism of *Rottman*: The readiness of the Court to dare take a further step in this 'holy' domain of the member states could easily have been foreseen.[32] Since *Micheletti*, the Court has shown itself prepared to influence nationality laws in the case of a clear breach of Union law.

Before the activism of the court,[33] however, doctrine is divided (Jessurun d'Oliveira et al. 2011). For some, the limits to a member state's ability to strip its nationals of access to European citizenship rights is essential for explaining the *ratio* of the institution of Union citizenship (its federal vocation) as well as the court's well established case-law; for others, it is a form of 'impérialism communautaire' (Ruzié 1993). While some claim the 'judicial avantguardism' is to be praised, for others, in this very case-law 'the court is persisting in its judicial error' (Jessurun d'Oliveira 2011, p. 9).

There is also an institutional twist to this doctrinal divide: While the case-law of the European Court of Justice moves in the direction of making nationality matters a mixed competence, it simultaneously constitutes a dissenting voice when compared to the positions expressed by Member States, the Commission and the European Parliament that all seem to endorse the traditional reading of nationality matters being *domaine réservé*. In fact, the Commission has systematically taken the perspective of defending member state prerogative in nationality matters. Also the European Parliament has taken this view more often than not. The advocates of the opposed view, instead, insists on the decoupling of national and European citizenship: European citizenship is not merely 'derivative' (Maastricht) but then also 'complementary' (Treaty of Amsterdam) and, after Lisbon, EU citizenship is 'additional' (Geogiadou 2015, p. xix).

In this divided environment, it seems that the *prima facie* assurance that Brexit loss provision would not fall within the remit of Union law (since loss would only happen simultaneously to the UK's exit from the Union) is a bit shaken: 'By reason of its nature and its consequences'[34] Brexit puts Union citizens of exclusively British nationality at risk of being stripped of their Union membership status in a way that might fall within the ambit of EU law.

If this is so, decisive are the possibilities to challenge the loss provision. Are there any venues for challenging the loss provision as such in which the consequentialist interpretation in *Rottman* might play a role?

Challenging the loss of rights, where *Rottman* may be relevant, is possible, but loss of status is another matter. A possibility is the right of standing of a British second country national living in a member state who wishes to challenge the loss of status before a domestic court in the country of residence. One such case might involve for instance the British citizen who, on the basis of the status of Union citizenship, holds local political office of which (s)he will be discharged following Brexit. Dealing with such a case, a national court may refer to the European Court of Justice. Were the European Court of Justice to express itself in a preliminary ruling on the legitimacy of the loss of status as such, *Rottman*'s *ratio decidendi* would apply. The Court might find the loss of Union citizenship to be inadmissible since it previously ruled that a 'national provision governing nationality [that] restricts the Union citizen without a legitimate interest and/or in a disproportionate manner' was such that the provision shall be put aside. Could it mean that Union citizenship ought to be recognised to the former Union citizenship? Ought (s)he be naturalised though a procedure of naturalisation by declaration (not by application, which would be open to all second country nationals anyway)? Could the local politician continue to stand in elections?

During the *interregnum*, that is, after invoking Article 50 but before exiting, would a British first country national be refused right of standing before a national (UK) court to challenge the loss provision? Albeit politically remote, would not the Court be free to activate a preliminary ruling procedure? If the European Court of Justice could be called into question, would it not be able to rely on its *Rottman* doctrine? In *Rottman* the crucial point was the loss of Union citizenship as such. Brexit would '*by reason of its nature and consequences*' almost tautologically place many 'in a position capable of causing [them] to lose the status conferred by Art. 17 EC.' Were this line of reasoning followed, the European Court of Justice could open the constitutional dispute we referred to in Chapter 4: Union citizenship or Article 50 – *aut aut*? This certainly raises the question if the Court in Luxembourg is the authority to ask to fashion the constitutional arrangement in the European *respublica composita* (Beaud 2009, p. 222) or if this role ought not to be better allocated to democratically elected authorities.

Once closed, the *interregnum*, and this far-off window of legal opportunity in which the European Court of Justice could vindicate decoupling, there are no procedural venues through which former Union citizens could challenge their loss of status. International law provides that states are obliged to leave the possibility to citizens deprived of citizenship (no matter if it causes statelessness, and no matter if caused by administrative decision or by the workings of the law) the right to challenge the provision in court. But channels for challenging the loss of status following withdrawal from the Union are not explicitly provided for neither in European law, nor in domestic law. Were no venues open to challenge the loss of Union citizenship for British citizens, we would need to conclude that Article 50 introduces surreptitiously an unchallengeable new ground for loss of the status. It cannot be ruled out that, in keeping with international law, such an unchallengeable provision of loss might, after all, qualify as arbitrary.

6.5   Enacting Union Citizenship

Before the involuntary loss of status imposed on millions of British citizens on both sides of the border, it seems that the possibilities of challenging this provision are quite limited and unattractive.

The EU organs cannot by themselves push for decoupling. There is not much the Commission can do to hinder an exiting state from stripping those nationals who belong exclusively to the exiting state of the Union's *status civitatis*. There is a slight possibility that the European Court of Justice might push in this direction, on the basis of the *Rottman* doctrine. Doing so would pose serious risks: If impetus to decouple Union citizenship from nationality derives from a decision by the European Court of Justice it can be attacked on democratic grounds and be found at odds with the current constitutional arrangement of the EU. The Court of Justice could exploit this window of opportunity, but only at the cost of showing itself uninterested in obeying to democratic standards and perhaps also disposed to perturb the constitutional arrangement.

The EU member states are in a better position to further decoupling in order to save the status for (at least some) British nationals. Some scholars have suggested they use this position to create 'a form of Union citizenship unmediated by any prior national citizenship' (Morgan 2016). Of course, there is the impervious road of re-drafting the Treaties but, given its political improbability and legal impracticality, I shall put this option aside. Nonetheless, the Council may help to coordinate member states wishing to ease naturalisation for locally residing British citizens, automatically transform the status of permanent residents into third country national long-term residents, or in other ways seek to either maintain the status of Union citizen for post-European Brits or to freeze rights. Whereas a member state is not free to engage in mass naturalisation on its own initiative (lest it violates the principle of sincere cooperation), coordinated member states are not liable to objections about undemocratic or unconstitutional behaviour to the same extent as a court.

Last but not least, there is another way to save the status that has hitherto been overlooked: Union citizens themselves might push for decoupling. This can be done in two different ways.

The first way consists in activating a citizens' initiative (Art. 11 § 4 TEU). If a million EU citizens, coming from at least seven member states, sign an initiative and the Commission decides to propose legislation as a result of it, the status of Union citizenship may well prove to be 'destined to become the fundamental status' of nationals of (former) member states as well. It is politically remote that, first, Union citizens show much solidarity with *remainers*; and second, that the Commission, who, in its role of guardian of the Treatises, generally endorses the traditional reading of nationality matters being *domaine réservé* (see above 6.3.), would favour decoupling. As a matter of law, it remains possible for Union citizens to help British citizens who have been stripped of the status they once shared. There are constitutionally foreseen venues, so unsettling of the arrangement would not be necessary. The democratic quality of such an initiative would not be challenged as it emerges bottom-up: It is the very role of citizens within a polity to be mindful about the primordial political right of defining the *demos*.

Moreover, the citizenship initiative introduced by the Treaty of Lisbon is itself a supranational political instrument. The citizens' initiative introduced by the Treaty of Lisbon was framed specifically for giving voice to cross-national political concerns on the basis of a political conception of EU citizenship: The *Regulation of the EU Parliament and the Council on the citizens' initiative* from 2010 emblematically fixes the threshold at '0.2% of the *population.*' Also, there would have been no point in setting different thresholds for different countries if the petition names were to stand merely for national interests rather than a cross-national opinion.

It is one of the elements that allows to make the claim that Union citizenship does not merely consist in mutually recognised privileges, but also in supranational political rights. Using it to save the supranational political rights of citizens that risk losing these – because of decisions possibly made by a member state government following a non-binding referendum in which the most affected were effectively disenfranchised[35] – strengthens the claim that an initiative on decoupling with the purpose of saving the status as Union citizens for British resident in the Union ought to be taken seriously even by a Commission otherwise reluctant to move in this direction. Were the Commission to take up the challenge, it would find that the *Rottman* doctrine of the European Court of Justice would go a long way in doing the job of explaining why loss of Union citizenship cannot be imposed unilaterally by one's (ex member) state of nationality.

There are solutions that would enable the Union citizenry to *enact* its citizenship, as Engin Isin has called it (Isin and Saward 2015), by becoming politically active and willing to contest arbitrary exercises of power.

Another way to enact citizenship is the second way for Union citizens to push for decoupling. The two ways are not alternative and can be pursued in parallel. Given the passivity of the non-British public before Brexit, the disenfranchised British citizens, with no other member state nationality to rely on, that are being deprived of the status of Union citizens, in a way that will also result, in a number of member states, in losing their local political citizenship, may petition the European Parliament to ask for a decoupling that will allow them to keep their status. The Parliament, even though sometimes reticent towards to the activism of the European Court of Justice in nationality and citizenship matters, is, contrarily to the Commission, the institution potentially most favourable to decoupling: It has on several occasions viewed its own mandate as representing the *population* of the Union and not merely the sum of nationals of member states.[36] Petitioning Parliament does not amount to political initiative, but it could lead to a declaration by the Parliament inviting the Council and the Commission to provide for the loss of status. Since it would only concern former Union citizens and not all residents, there are chances a plea might be taken seriously.

This way to 'save' the citizenship of deprived British nationals remains open after Brexit occurs. All residents may petition the Parliament and, as we have seen, there are reasons for believing that British citizens currently resident in the Union will see their residence rights frozen.

NOTES

1. European Parliament, *OJ* C 77/53, 19 March 1984.
2. A terminological remark is needed: There are many expressions relating to loss of *status civitatis*: loss, quasi-loss (or *ex tunc* declaration of invalidity), deprivation, lapse, withdrawal, renunciation. Deprivation or withdrawal is

usually an administrative measure by the competent authorities whilst lapse or *ex lege* loss happens automatically by operation of the law. Renunciation is voluntary. See Glossary Eudo-citizenship, available at http://eudo-citizen ship.eu/databases/citizenship-glossary (last accessed 30 October 2016). See Weis 1979; De Groot 2015, at 10.

3. The UK supreme court refused the permission to appeal on the grounds of purely domestic law, leaving all EU citizens of UK nationality residing in other member states disenfranchised in the referendum: UKSC 2016/0105. See e.g. Ziegler 2016.

4. See Chapter 2. The ability to disconnect member state nationality from EU citizenship, although confirmed in *Kaur*, is much more difficult for the member states to use after *Rottmann*.

5. My italics.

6. BVerfG, 2 BvE 2/08, 30/06/09, § 350.

7. See Chapter 2. This choice give rise to concerns both for the political legitimacy of the construct and for legal foreseeability in certain hard cases: Mindus 2008; Mindus and Goldoni 2012. For a comparative reading with federal settings, see Schönberger 2005.

8. See the research results of the ILEC project: Carrera Nunez, De Groot 2015; De Groot and Vonk 2016.

9. The UNDHR is here reminiscent of the Decree of Adolf Hitler of 25 November 1941 that determined loss *ex lege* of status for Jewish citizens of Germany.

10. For a general overview, UN Human Rights Council (12009), *Human Rights and Arbitrary Deprivation of Nationality: Report of the Secretary-General*, 14 December, A/HRC/13/34.

11. These principles include that a loss of citizenship requires (1) firm legal basis; (2) may not be enacted retroactively; (3) in case of the introduction of a new ground of loss, a reasonable transitory provision has to be made to avoid an individual losing his nationality due to an act that had already started before the introduction of the new ground for loss; (4) a legal provision regarding the acquisition of nationality may not be repealed with retroactivity; (5) the principle *tempus regit factum* applies; (6) loss provisions must be easily accessible and predicable; (7) the ground given for deprivation must be proportional; (8) provisions may not be discriminatory; (9) it must be possible to challenge the application of loss provisions in court. Full list and analysis in De Groot 2015, at 9–39.

12. See Chapter 2.

13. *Mario Vicente Micheletti and others v Delegación del Gobierno en Cantabria*, Case C-369/90 § 10.

14. Case C-315/08, *Janko Rottman v. Freistaat Bayern*, § 51.

15. Among those who have insisted on this, there is the Institute for Public Policy Research that maintained in a recent report that a fundamental

reform of the UK citizenship policy is required after Brexit. See Murray 2016.

16. One reading of this term may be those having exercised 'treaty rights' or are in process of doing so.

17. Notice, for example, that 2/3 flopped the Danish citizenship test recently. The test includes questions such as which Danish restaurant has three Michelin stars. It is not Noma.

18. See note 21.

19. Belgium, Cyprus, Denmark, Finland, France, Ireland, Malta, Netherlands, Spain, Sweden. The details of these rules vary considerably in procedure (lapse vs. withdrawl), personal scope (naturalised, foreign-born citizens or all), statelessness (only for dual citizens or not), age, and connected sanctions.

20. Given the large number of British nationals currently living in Spain, it is worth recalling that Spain does enforce such a ban.

21. *Nottebohm* 6 April 1955, *Liechtenstein v. Guatemala*, CIJ Recueil, at 23 ff. Glazer 1955; Bastide 1956; Maury 1958; Weis 1979, esp. 176–181 and 318–321. A national of a member state who is also a national of a non-member state is a EU citizen regardless of social ties or place of residence: since the ruling in *Mario Vicente Micheletti v Delegación del Gobierno en Cantabria* (Case C-369/90), the European Court of Justice favours a formalist reading that distances itself from the doctrine of 'genuine link.' See Chapter 2.

22. http://www.spiegel.de/politik/deutschland/brexit-sigmar-gabriel-for dert-doppelte-staatsbuergerschaft-fuer-junge-briten-a-1101010.html (last accessed 30 October 2016).

23. Opinion of AG Poiares Maduro in Case C-135/08, *Rottman* [2010] ECR I-01449.

24. In 2006 the Council of Europe adopted a new specific *Convention of the Avoidance of Statelessness in Relation to State Succession* that establishes that the successor state should grant nationality to certain nationals of the pre-decessor State if they would otherwise become stateless. This specific group includes those who are habitually resident in the successor state, those with a legal bond through federal citizenship, those born there or having their last habitual residence there before leaving the predecessor state. It is ratified only by Austria, Hungary and the Netherland.

25. It has been suggested that the *Ruiz Zambrano* doctrine on 'genuine sub-stance' would be relevant to allow decoupling: it would: replicate the emanci-patory move of *Van Gend en Loos* – to liberate individuals from the preferences of their states. De-coupling would signify a constitutional recognition that rights acquired as European citizens really are 'fundamental': integral to individual personhood and therefore inscribed into the deep structure of an autonomous EU legal order (Dawson and Augenstein 2016).

26. Case C-34/09, *Ruiz Zambrano* EU:C:2011:124. The Court supplemented the protection of the status of Union citizenship with the requirement that the substance of rights attached to the status be enjoyed. The ECJ resorted to the 'substance' of European citizenship to ground the entitlement of a third country national to reside and work in Belgium as the father care-taker of two children who had been born nationals of Belgium in order to avoid statelessness that would have followed from being born by Colombian nationals who did not reside in Colombia (Colombia being a country applying *ius soli* quite strictly): 'Article 20 TFEU precludes national measures which have the effect of depriving citizens of the Union of the genuine enjoyment of the substance of the rights conferred by virtue of their status as citizens of the Union. A refusal to grant a right of residence to a third country national with dependent minor children in the Member State where those children are nationals and reside, [. . .] has such an effect.'

27. See Case C-256/2011, *Dereci* EU:C:2011:734; Case C-434/09, *Shirley McCarthy* EU:C:2011:277.

28. It does not cover lesser interferences such as with the mere desire to keep a family together in a given member state. See Joint Cases 356/11 and 357/11, *O, S* EU:C:2012:776, § 52; Case C-87/12, *Ymeraga* EU:C:2013:291, § 38. Also see Case C-86/12, *Alokpa* EU:C:2013:645.

29. Case C-135/08 *Janko Rottmann v Freistaat Bayern* [2010] ECR nyp, § 42.

30. In the case of *Kaur* (16 Case C-192/99 The Queen v Secretary of State for the Home Department, ex parte: Manjit Kaur [2001] ECR I-01237), the British nationality rules were examined by the European Court of Justice. In that case a third country national who was recognised by the UK as citizen of the UK and Colonies but did not fall within the personal scope of citizens entitled to right to abode, could not rely on her Union citizenship. The European Court of Justice held, in that case, that the declaration on nationality of the UK 'did not have the effect of depriving any person who did not satisfy the definition of a national of the UK of rights to which that person might be entitled under Community law. The consequence was rather that such rights never arose in the first place for such a person.' *Kaur* is a case of quasi loss, *Rottman* a case of loss.

31. See ILEC Guidelines IV.5.c. and V.a.; De Groot 2015, at 35.

32. On *Rottman*, and for extensive comments on why it was not a judgment 'out of the blue' but rather consistent with previous activism of the European Court of Justice: see http://eudo-citizenship.eu/commen taries/254-has-the-european-court-of-justice-challenged-member-state-sovereignty-in-nationality-law?start=1 (last accessed 30 October 2016).

33. The case-law of the European Court of Justice generally has been pointing towards avantguardism of pushing EU citizenship beyond the merely economically motivated concept. See cases such as *Baubast* (C-413/99),

Martínez-Sala (C-85/96), *Grzelczyk* (C-184/99), *Garcia Avello* (C-148/02) and *Bidar* (C-209/03).

34. De Groot calls this doctrine 'an even more sensational construct' that the claim made by the Advocate General Maduro that since Rottman was born Austrian and made use of his EU citizenship and his freedom of movement when moving to Germany, the case ought not to be considered a 'purely internal one' (De Groot 2010).

35. See note 3.

36. For example, during the 2007 intergovernmental conference, Italy did not approve the new composition of the European Parliament. On this incident, see Manzella 2008. The proposal voted by the European Parliament had used a formula based on resident *population* rather than 'citizenship' (i.e. nationality). It would have left Italy with 72 seats compared to 73 for the UK, 74 for France (that had historically had the same weight as Italy). This dispute led to Declaration 4 attributing the extra seat to Italy and to Declaration 57 on the definition of citizenship.

REFERENCES

Bastide, S. (1956) 'L'affaire Nottebohm devant la Cour Internationale de Justice', 45 *Revue critique de droit international privé* 607–633.

Beaud, O. (2009) *Théorie de la fédération*, Paris: Puf.

Carrera Nuñez, S., De Groot, G.-R. (eds.) (2015) *European Citizenship at the Crossroads. The Role of the European Union on Loss and Acquisition of Nationality*, Oisterwijk: Wolf.

Davis, G. (2011) 'The Entirely Conventional Supremacy of Union Citizenship and Rights', Commentary in 'Has the European Court of Justice Challenged Member State Sovereignty in Nationality Law?' Forum Debates EUDO, available at http://eudo-citizenship.eu/commentaries/citizenship-forum/citizenship-forum-cat/254-has-the-european-court-of-justice-challenged-member-state-sovereignty-in-nationality-law?showall=&start=1 (last accessed 30 October 2016).

Dawson, M., Augenstein, D. (2016) 'After Brexit: Time for a Further Decoupling of European and National Citizenship?' *VerfBlog*, 14 July 2016, available at http://verfassungsblog.de/brexit-decoupling-european-national-citizenship/ (last accessed 30 October 2016).

De Groot, G.R. (2004) 'Towards a European Nationality Law', *Electronic Journal of Comparative Law* 8, available at http://www.ejcl.org/83/art83-4.html (last accessed 30 October 2016).

De Groot, G.R. (2010) 'Invloed van het Unierecht op het nationaliteitsrecht van de Lidstaten: Overwegingen over de Janko Rottman-beslissing van het Europees Hof van Justitie', 5/6 *Asiel & Migratierecht*, 293–300.

De Groot, G.-R. (2015) 'Survey on the Rules on Loss of Nationality in International Treatises and Case Law', in S. Carrera Nuñez, G.-R. De Groot (eds.) *European Citizenship at the Crossroads. The Role of the European Union on Loss and Acquisition of Nationality*, Oisterwijk: Wolf Legal Publishers.

De Groot, G.-R., Vonk, O. (2016) *International Standards on Nationality Law: Text, Cases and Materials*, Oisterwijk: Wolf Legal Publishers.

De Mars, S., Murray, C., O'Donoghue, A., Warwick, B. (2016) 'Brexit-ing Northern Ireland: The Challenges Ahead', *DeliBlog*, Blog entry from 11 July 2016, available at https://delilawblog.wordpress.com/2016/07/11/sylvia-de-mars-colin-murray-aoife-odonoghue-ben-warwick-brexit-ing-northern-ireland-the-challenges-ahead/ (last accessed 30 October 2016).

Dzankic, J. (2016) 'Brexit and Citizenship', Report EUDO blog entry 27 June 2016, available at http://eudo-citizenship.eu/news/citizenship-news/1636-brexit-and-citizenship (last accessed 30 October 2016).

Evans, A.C. (1991) 'Nationality Law and European Integration', 16 *European Law Review* 190.

Føllesdal, A. (1993) 'Third Country Nationals as Euro-Citizens – The Case Defended', in D. Smith, S. Wright (eds.) *Whose Europe? The Turn Towards Democracy*, Blackwell: London, 104–122.

Fransman, L. (2011) *Fransman's British Nationality Law*, 3rd ed., West Sussex: Bloomsbury Professional.

Geogiadou, Z. (2015) 'Foreword', in S. Carrera Nuñez, G.-R. De Groot (eds.) *European Citizenship at the Crossroads. The Role of the European Union on Loss and Acquisition of Citizenship* (ILEC), Oisterwijk: Wolf Legal Publishers.

Glazer, J.H. (1955) 'Affaire Nottebohm (Lichtenstein v. Guatemala), A Critique', 44 *Georgetown Law Journal* 1955/56 313–325.

Glossary Eudo-Citizenship available at http://eudo-citizenship.eu/databases/citizenship-glossary (last accessed 30 October 2016).

Hall, S. (1995) *Nationality, Migration Rights and Citizenship of the Union*, Leiden: Martinus Nijhoff.

Hall, S. (1996) 'Loss of Union Citizenship in Breach of Fundamental Rights', 21 *European Law Review* 488.

Hall, S. (2001) 'Determining the Scope *ratione personae* of European Citizenship: Customary International Law Prevails for Now', 28(3) *Legal Issues of Economic Integration*, 355–360.

Howarth, D.J. (1994) 'The Compromise on Denmark and the Treaty on the European Union: A Legal and Political Analysis', 31 *Common Market Law Review* 4, 765–805.

Isin, E., Saward, M. (2015) *Enacting European Citizenship*, Cambridge: CUP.

Jessurun d'Oliveira, H.U. (2011) 'Court of Justice of the European Union: Decision of 2 March 2010, Case C-315/08, Janko Rottman v. Freistaat

Bayern Case Note 1 Decoupling Nationality and Union Citizenship?', 7 *European Constitutional Law Review* 1, 138 ff.

Jessurun d'Oliveira, H.U., De Groot, G.-R., Seling, A. (2011) 'Court of Justice of the European Union: Decision of 2 March 2010, Case C-315/08, Janko Rottman v. Freistaat Bayern Case Note 1 Decoupling Nationality and Union Citizenship? Case Note 2 The Consequences of the Rottmann Judgment on Member State Autonomy – The European Court of Justice's Avant-Gardism in Nationality Matters', 7 *European Constitutional Law Review* 1, 138–160.

Kochenov, D. (2016) *EU Citizenship and Withdrawals from the Union: How Inevitable is the Radical Downgrading of Rights?*, LEQS Paper No. 111/2016, available at http://www.lse.ac.uk/europeanInstitute/LEQS%20Discussion%20Paper%20Series/LEQSPaper111.pdf (last accessed 30 October 2016).

Kotalakidis, N. (2000) *Von der nationalen Staatsangehörigkeit zur Unionsbürgerschaft. Die Person und das Gemeinwesen*, Baden: Nomos.

Manzella, A. (2008) 'Un trattato necessitato', in F. Bassanini, G. Tiberi (eds.) *Le nuove istituzioni europee. Commento al Trattato di Lisbona*, Bologna: Il Mulino. 438 ff.

Marescaux, M.H. (1984) 'Nationalité et statut personnel dans les instruments internationaux des Nations Unies', in M. Verwilghen (ed.) *Nationalité et statut personnel: Leur interaction dans les traités internationaux et dans les législations nationales*, Bruxelles: Bruylant.

Maury, J. (1958) 'L'arrêt Nottebohm et la condition de nationalité effective', 23 *Zeitschrift für ausländisches und internationales Privatrecht* 515–534.

Mindus, P. (2008) 'Europeanisation of Citizenship within the EU: Perspectives and Ambiguities, Jean Monnet Series of Working Paper', available at https://iris.unito.it/retrieve/handle/2318/82213/11168/MINDUS%20JM%20WP%20in%20rete.pdf (last accessed 30 October 2016).

Mindus, P., Goldoni, M. (2012) 'Between Democracy and Nationality: Citizenship Policies in the Lisbon Ruling', 18 *European Public Law* 2, 351–371.

Morgan, G. (2016) 'Union Citizenship for UK Citizens', EUDO Forum Debates Freedom of Movement Under Attack: Is it Worth Defending as the Core of EU Citizenship?, available at http://eudo-citizenship.eu/commentaries/citizenship-forum/citizenship-forum-cat/1586-freedom-of-movement-under-attack-is-it-worth-defending-as-the-core-of-eu-citizenship?showall=&start=11 (last accessed 8 November 2016).

Murray, C. (2016) 'Becoming One of Us: Reforming the UK's Citizenship System for a Competitive, Post-Brexit World, Report for the Institute for Public Policy Research', available at http://www.ippr.org/publications/becoming-one-of-us (last accessed 30 October 2016).

Ruzié, D. (1993) 'Nationalité, effectivité et droit communautaire', 97 *Revue générale de droit international public* 107–120.

Schönberger, C. (2005) *Unionsbürger: Europas föderales Bürgerrecht in vergleichender Sicht*, Tübingen: Mohr.

Steinbeis, M. (2016) 'Nach dem Brexit-Referendum: ein Fast Track zur deutschen Staatsbürgerschaft für bedrohte Unionsbürger!', *VerfBlog*, 24 June 2016, available at http://verfassungsblog.de/brexit-fast-track-staatsbuergerschaft-unionsbuerger/ (last accessed 30 October 2016).

Tryfonidou, A. (2008) 'Reverse Discrimination in Purely Internal Situations: An Incongruity in a Citizens' Europe', 35 *Legal Issues of Economic Integration* 43.

Weis, P. (1979) *Nationality and Statelessness in International Law*, 2nd ed., London: Stevens & Sons.

Ziegler, R. (2016) 'The Referendum of the UK's EU Membership: No Legal Salve for its Disenfranchised Non-resident Citizens', *VerfBlog*, 21 June 2016 available at http://verfassungsblog.de/the-referendum-of-the-uks-eu-membership-no-legal-salve-for-its-disenfranchised-non-resident-citizens/ (last accessed 30 October 2016).

CHAPTER 7

Towards a Functionalist Reading of Union Citizenship

Abstract In this final chapter some conclusions as to the nature of Union citizenship are drawn. Union citizenship is found to constitute, as a reflection of the Union itself, a *status sui generis*. It consists of both supranational and transnational elements. Some parallels are also drawn to the way citizenship and interstate equality is framed in American constitutional case-law. Being clear about what European citizenship is helps us to resolve the constitutional dilemma formulated in Chapter 4: Do we need to choose between sacrificing EU citizens' rights or taking Article 50 seriously? The chapter shows why this is not the case.

Keywords European citizenship · Brexit · Freedom of movement · Right of residence · EU law · Migration law · International law · Interstate equality

No matter its shape, Brexit brings changes to the territorial scope of application of the Treatises. This impacts on what has been called one of the major achievements of EU integration: The citizenry of the Union. It will shrink in size, change in composition and some parts of it will be very exposed. Especially those individuals who have relied on free movement in making their life choices. Many are worried about losing residence rights and being subjected to a different migration status. The reduction of rights will affect not only British citizens but also European citizens in

© The Author(s) 2017
P. Mindus, *European Citizenship after Brexit*, Palgrave Studies in European Union Politics, DOI 10.1007/978-3-319-51774-2_7

the UK and their family members. On both sides of the emerging border there will be much insecurity. In many member states British nationals living there will also lose local political citizenship.

What is more is that, for the first time, European citizens face a collective and automatic lapse of status. Loss of citizenship *en masse*, by the automatic workings of the law, will affect all EU citizens of exclusively British nationality. It was long claimed that the only way to lose EU citizenship was by losing nationality. Brexit proves this wrong: Indirectly Article 50 adds a ground for losing Union citizenship. Legally speaking, this loss of citizenship is not voluntary: It is not fruit of (individual) renunciation. In the case of Brexit one may also make the political claim that it is involuntary because 48% expressed their will to remain; certain territories voted massively in favour of staying and non-resident UK citizens were disenfranchised.

In this theoretically grounded contribution we addressed some of the most urgent policy questions in the wake of Brexit: How to deal with Brits living in the rest of the EU, and other Europeans living in the UK. The inquiry started out by briefly outlining the history and the status of European citizenship (Chapter 2). Union citizenship was found to constitute, as a reflection of the Union itself, a *status civitatis sui generis*. It consists of both supranational and transnational types of entitlements. We took the issue to a deeper and more intriguing level by asking which rights can be frozen (Chapter 5) for different categories of people who, having made use of freedom of movement, are left in a legal limbo after Brexit, awaiting indication about how their position will be regulated in migration and nationality law. This limbo was characterised by reference to a series of potential hard cases to come (Chapter 3). The complicated issue of competence in the area of Union citizenship was also addressed, in particular with reference to loss of the status. The various options were presented and the anticipated consequences for both the UK and EU states fleshed out. Venues for challenging the loss of status were also discussed (Chapter 6). What overall enabled the analysis was the functionalist theory of citizenship (Chapter 4).

The key finding is that while member states are in principle free to revoke the status of Union citizen, former member states are not unbounded in stripping Union citizens of their acquired territorial rights. The European Convention of Human Rights steps in and protects the residence rights of those lawfully residing in the territories covered by EU law at the moment of independence. Also, the supranational rights of

Union citizens being subjected to massive lapse of status can be vindicated by the citizenry of the Union.

Moreover, it was shown that the UK is not well-equipped to prevent instrumental use of multiple citizenships. Generally speaking, there is a tradition of tolerance towards multiple citizenship in the UK.

Policy suggestions were outlined. It was found that provisions on loss of citizenship need to be read in the light of the general principle of the UN Declaration of Human Rights banning arbitrary deprivation. International law has elaborated a series of guiding principles for framing arbitrary deprivation. These principles have to be observed not only if the loss or deprivation would cause statelessness, but in all cases where a person would be stripped of a citizenship. So Brexit loss provision would need to obey these principles.

Nationality law belongs to the *domaine réservé* but domestic choices are not neutral *vis-à-vis* Union citizenship. There may be incentives for the UK to adopt or modify domestic provisions in a way, however, that would need to pay 'due regard' to European law. Under the banner of taking back control, the UK may be spurred to restrict pervasive (ab)use of multiple citizenships and/or to tolerate it only in some cases; and/or to penalise instrumental naturalisation by its own nationals living in other member states. There are many ways to do so. But such incentives would need to be resisted for quite some time. Indeed, after having invoked Article 50 and throughout the negotiation phase, the UK could not:

- Pass domestic nationality provisions easing naturalisation only for some EU citizens since it would violate the principle of non-discrimination
- Change domestic nationality provisions with the effect of barring, or rendering more difficult or overly onerous, naturalisation of second country nationals since such a policy would violate the principle of legitimate expectations
- Fight instrumental naturalisation of its own nationals by stripping them of their British nationality and/or residence rights in case of naturalisation abroad
- Re-introduce additional criteria, such as the requirement of 'a genuine link' for people with more than one nationality
- Make applications for indefinite leave to remain harder to obtain

During this phase, European law would still hold and modifications to policies, including immigration and nationality law, may come to be scrutinised by the Union. Were the UK to modify its policy in ways incompatible with European law, it could be subjected to infringement procedure by the Commission and judicial review by the European Court of Justice. Overall, it would be detrimental to negotiations to harden UK nationality laws and/or immigration laws.

On the other hand, there are limits to what member states can do to both assist and deter British citizens from continuing living in the Union and eventually naturalising there. Rendering family reunification for British citizens harder, say, would violate the principle of legitimate expectations. Member states are also prevented from, say, naturalising Brits *en masse* because of the principle of sincere cooperation.

There are also a number of policies that all actors – EU institutions, member states and the UK – could adopt to make the transformation of second country nationals into third country nationals easier for Brits in the Union and for making the passage from being second country nationals to becoming simple foreigners under the British legal order for European citizens living in the UK. Chapter 6 dealt extensively with these different policy options. Here is a summarising scheme (Fig. 7.1): We are now in a position to answer those who fear the constitutional 'dilemma' referred to in Chapter 4. Does Brexit imply that we need to make a choice between sacrificing EU citizens' rights on the altar of the referendum or sacrificing the will of Brexiters on the altar of the rights of Union citizens? No, we do not: The dilemma is apparent.

On one hand, we do not need to sacrifice Union citizens' rights to allow Brexit. The supranational rights of Union citizens being subjected to massive lapse of status can be vindicated by the citizenry of the Union: By petitioning and organising a citizens' initiative the possibility is given to the citizenry of the Union to enact itself as a 'body politic' and call for the 'inter-citizenship' distinctive of any *composite republic* so as to save the status of those who are placed 'in a position capable of causing them to lose the status conferred by Article 17 EC.'

On the other hand, we need not sacrifice the will of Brexiters to save residence rights. Many are thus worried in vain. More precisely, the reasons of worry here are more of a political nature, not strictly legal since law does offer remedial solutions. Even if Union citizenship is lost due to changed legal status of a territory, the European Court of Human Rights steps in and protects the residence rights of those lawfully residing in the territories covered by European law at the moment of independence. This will be so at least until the EU adheres to the European Convention of Human Rights,

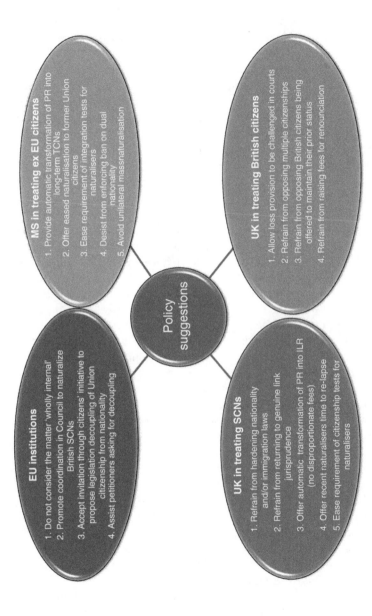

Fig. 7.1 Policy suggestions for EU institutions in treating Union citizenship after Brexit, for Member states (MS) in treating British citizens (former Union citizens), and for the United Kingdom in treating second country nationals (SCNs) as well as its own citizens in reference to their loosing European citizenship

an idea that lost traction in the wake of the ECJ's *Opinion 2/13* from 2014. It seems that a person can enjoy certain rights commonly associated with Union citizenship even in the case the status as such is no longer held.

Some Brexite(e)rs, unsurprisingly, will understand this to be a form of Hotel California doctrine, according to which 'you can check out any time you want but you can never leave.' This impression is, however, mistaken since the *Kurić* formula would 'cement' the existing residence rights, but would not extend the applicability of EU law to the territories exiting the Union. However, the politically uncomfortable fact remains that the doctrine allows freezing of residence rights. Freezing is possible no matter if states decide to share sovereignty or to jealously rein it in within national borders.

Is it then a *coup*? As emphasised in Chapter 4, to some, Brexit offers a constitutional test: If rights are saved and decoupling occurs, shifting citizens' entitlement to jointly decide about membership in the polity from the national to the European level would 'amount to a *coup d'état*' (Dawson and Augenstein 2016). Would such a freezing of rights mean that Union citizenship deprives Article 50 of its *effet utile*?

There is no coup, to be sure: For Brexit to yield anything like a constitutionally jeopardising form of decoupling between nationality and Union citizenship it would require extremely fanciful inventiveness of behalf of the Commission; or, the European Court of Justice would need to be sparked to open the constitutional contention over the loss of the status by referring to the *Rottman* doctrine in the case – in my view remote, albeit technically not impossible – of a first country national, that is, a British citizen not having made use of his or her right to free movement, challenging the loss provision before a British court which requires a preliminary ruling, during the *interregnum*, that is, after the invocation of Article 50 but before effectuating the exit.

Nonetheless, it is possible for Brexit to yield a form of decoupling between nationality and Union citizenship that would not, however, be constitutionally jeopardising. Such a solution would need to rely on the enactment of Union citizenship and/or adoption by member states of a naturalisation procedure for former Union citizens that would not violate the general principles of European law.

Many claimed in the wake of the referendum, that Union citizenship is not a 'federalist element' of the European integration project since Union citizens enjoy their 'fundamental status' and 'citizenship rights' only *Solange* (so long) as the member state of which they happen to have the nationality does not invoke Article 50. Has Brexit shown this to be the case? Is Union citizenship, after all, nothing but a concession made by the Masters of the Treaties that can be called back at political convenience? Is EU citizenship somehow 'meaningless'?

A positive implication of adopting the functionalist theory is that answers to these questions are of no consequence for the analysis conducted. It does not matter for the functionalist theory whether the citizenship is 'real' or a case of rhetoric. The theory is only committed to the fact that citizenship is a status, putative or not. The theory is agnostic towards 'thick' concepts associated with citizenship such as identity and recognition. This is due to the fact that it is not a theory suggesting a conception of citizenship. There are arguably many such conceptions, the pros and cons of which have been debated in great detail over the last decades by citizenship scholars (Mindus 2014).

The functionalist theory offers a *concept* of citizenship, not a *conception*. The concept of citizenship that the theory develops only requires a very minimal ontological commitment: That *status civitatis* is, conceptually speaking, a middle-term. As such, it is not true, nor false. As such, it does not 'correspond' to any empirical fact. It can, nonetheless, be investigated from an empirical perspective. There does not need to be anything 'out there' to which the concept corresponds for it to work. What is required of *status civitatis* is to connect grounds for acquisition and loss with legal positions. This characterisation does not only fit the legal facts. It is fully able to explain the constitutional dimension of citizenship policy. No ontological commitments to people's identity or ability to identify with others are needed for this purpose. The theory is in line with the tradition of Scandinavian legal realism, a *corpus* of philosophical literature concerning this very point that has too often been neglected by legal scholars to their detriment.[1]

In keeping with this tradition, there is no need to believe that the legal concepts used somehow exist to provide insightful analysis into how they work. As Alf Ross famously argued in relation to the concept of ownership, it might be the case that it is in reality a meaningless word, a form of rhetoric, without changing the fact that, by looking at how it connects the *conditioning facts* and the *conditional consequences* in the law, we can understand perfectly well how the concept works – *et pour cause*, scrutinise it critically. I submit that the same is true for citizenship. By treating it as a middle-term – 'a technique of presentation' (Ross 1957, p. 821) or 'a vehicle of inference' (Lindahl 2004, p. 182) – it is possible to investigate both the *conditioning facts* (here: modes of acquisition and loss of the status) and the *conditional consequences* (here: entitlements connected to the status); then, to test whether they fit one another. The functionalist theory helps us to test the internal consistency of the status, and indicate under which conditions the loss of *status civitatis* is legitimate. Being a conceptual channel, *status civitatis* can be more or less capable of providing connection. The theory allows for critical analysis without subscribing to any specific substantial, 'thick' normative conception.

Is the post-Brexit loss of status illegitimate? As seen in Chapter 4, whether the loss is legitimate depends on the type of entitlements the status is connected to. According to the correlation thesis, legitimacy is dictated by fittingness of criteria (for acquisition and loss) to content. If content of the status is constituted by 'special rights' or mutually recognised privileges, unilateral imposition of loss of the kind that Brexit involves would be legitimate. If content of the status is constituted by supranational political rights that are as such generative of something else than that which generated it, unilateral imposition of loss of this kind would be illegitimate. Put differently, if supranational political rights constitute the content of the status, its loss is not only 'involuntary' in the technical sense (not fruit of renunciation) but also in the moral-political sense (not grounded on will). The answer to the question 'who gets to withdraw supranational entitlements?' cannot be any member state that so wishes. *A fortiori,* this authority cannot lie with a former member state, who would then have the authority to take away supranational entitlements to political participation in a Union of which it is no longer part.

Union citizenship consists of both categories: It comprises special rights grounded on mutual recognition as well as supranational political rights. The first kind of entitlements allows aggregation of member states. The second type of entitlements allows association of member states. Aggregation sums reciprocal state interests, defined by borders. Association produces common interests of individuals across borders. Consular protection is an example of the first kind. Citizens' initiative is an example of the second kind. Since the intension of Union citizenship is constituted in this way, a state that exits can legitimately withdraw some entitlements, but not others. However, such a solution is not technically feasible because the status – in a way characteristic of middle-terms of this kind – 'constitutes a bundle, the value of which depends on incorporating components [...that] jointly accomplishes a synergic effect' (Lindahl 2004, p. 199).

The intension of Union citizenship as a 'bundle' explains the 'miracle' which Poiares Maduro speaks of in the opinion cited in *incipit* to this book, taken from his *Opinion* on the *Rottman* case: '[T]hat is the miracle of Union citizenship: It strengthens the ties between us and our States (in so far as we are European citizens precisely because we are nationals of our States) and, at the same time, it emancipates us from them (in so far as we are now citizens beyond States).'

Some contents of Union citizenship strengthen the ties between us and our States insofar as they are privileges that we enjoy abroad. Some contents of Union citizenship emancipate us from our *Staatsangehörigkeit*, by constituting an interstate community in which we stand in relation one with another *notwithstanding* the states to which we belong.

As Wittgenstein recalls in his *Lecture on Ethics*, the truth is, of course, that the scientific way of looking at a fact is not the way to look at it as a miracle. From the scientific perspective, the 'miracle' is, to be precise, the effect of an unsettling asymmetry in the construction of the key dimensions of the *status civitatis*. The intension does not rim well with the extension. If the consistency of the status is to be raised, extension will need to follow intension. Member states are currently too free in managing a status that does not reflect *solely* on their members. Maintaining the link between national and European citizenship provides a strong argument for common European standards with regard to criteria determining acquisition and loss of Union citizenship through the nationality laws of member states. While prospects of instituting European conditionality for loss of the status are weak, Brexit offers a possibility for the citizenry of the Union to enact its citizenship.

Most 'private citizens' around the Union worry about their transnational rights of free movement and connected entitlements, their portable right not to be discriminated against as they move across borders, which is the European equivalent to the American doctrine of interstate equality, developed to protect the right to interstate travel.[2] These same individuals are also *citoyens* in a different meaning: They also enjoy local and supranational political citizenship in virtue of the same status.

It is well worth recalling that the US Supreme Court has dwelt on the link between equal protection, right to interstate travel and citizenship in a quite instructive way: In *Saenz* from 1995, the Court linked the horizontal protection of rights of the newly arrived in a state to their federal political capacity; that 'citizens have two political capacities, one state and one federal' adds special force to their claim that they are to be treated on the same footing as the other citizens.[3] Interstate equality, a horizontal bond among 'private citizens' thus relies on the fact that all citizens are equal in their federal political capacity, which constitutes a vertical link between the political community and *its* members. In this perspective, safeguarding the possibility of enacting citizenship is a crucial aspect of citizenship, of which horizontal citizenship is a reflection. This is so because citizenship in its political meaning constitutes membership of the kind that Justice Cardozo had in mind when he famously claimed that 'the people of the several states must sink or swim together.'[4]

NOTES

1. It has been suggested to me that the point is compatible also with, for example, Quinean explications of terms. The reference to Scandinavian legal realism is to be preferred nonetheless since it is chronologically prior and that the point was developed in explicit reference to legal terms of art by the participants in the realist movement and members of the so-called Uppsala school.
2. See Strumia 2016.
3. *Saenz* n. 26 § 504, quoting *US Term Limits v Thornton* 1995.
4. *Baldwin v GAF Seelig, Inc.* 294 US 522 [1935] § 523.

REFERENCES

Dawson, M., Augenstein, D., 'After Brexit: Time for a Further Decoupling of European and National Citizenship?', *VerfBlog*, 14 July 2016, available at http://verfassungsblog.de/brexit-decoupling-european-national-citizenship/ (last accessed 30 October 2016).

Lindahl, L. (2004) 'Deduction and Justification in the Law. The Role of Legal Terms and Concepts', 17 *Ratio Juris* 182–202.

Mindus, P. (2014) *Cittadini e no. Forme e funzioni dell'inclusione e dell'esclusione*, Florence: Firenze University Press.

Ross, A. (1957) 'Tû-Tû', 70 *Harvard Law Review* 5, 812–825.

Strumia, F. (2016) 'Individual Rights, Interstate Equality, State Autonomy: European Horizontal Citizenship and it (lonely) Playground in Trans-Atlantic Perspective', in D. Kochenov (ed.) *Citizenship and Federalism: The Role of Rights*, Cambridge: CUP.

INDEX

© The Author(s) 2017
P. Mindus, *European Citizenship after Brexit*, Palgrave Studies
in European Union Politics, DOI 10.1007/978-3-319-51774-2